Overseas Bases
and US Strategy:
Optimising America's
Military Footprint

Jonathan Stevenson

T0384234

'US overseas basing is a much debated but little understood topic. This study offers a valuable guide to America's strategic challenges in a volatile world.'

– Hal Brands, Henry A. Kissinger Distinguished Professor of Global Affairs, Johns Hopkins School of Advanced International Studies

Overseas Bases and US Strategy:
Optimising America's Military Footprint

Jonathan Stevenson

IISS The International Institute for Strategic Studies

The International Institute for Strategic Studies

Arundel House | 6 Temple Place | London | WC2R 2PG | UK

First published August 2022 by **Routledge**
4 Park Square, Milton Park, Abingdon, Oxon, OX14 4RN

for **The International Institute for Strategic Studies**
Arundel House, 6 Temple Place, London, WC2R 2PG, UK
www.iiss.org

Simultaneously published in the USA and Canada by **Routledge**
52 Vanderbilt Avenue, New York, NY 10017

Routledge is an imprint of Taylor & Francis, an Informa Business

© 2022 The International Institute for Strategic Studies

DIRECTOR-GENERAL AND CHIEF EXECUTIVE Dr John Chipman
SERIES EDITOR Dr Benjamin Rhode
EDITOR Dr Jeffrey Mazo
ASSISTANT EDITOR Gregory Brooks
EDITORIAL Laura Priest, Jill Lally
PRODUCTION Alessandra Beluffi
COVER ARTWORK James Parker

The International Institute for Strategic Studies is an independent centre for research, information and debate on the problems of conflict, however caused, that have, or potentially have, an important military content. The Council and Staff of the Institute are international and its membership is drawn from almost 100 countries. The Institute is independent and it alone decides what activities to conduct. It owes no allegiance to any government, any group of governments or any political or other organisation. The IISS stresses rigorous research with a forward-looking policy orientation and places particular emphasis on bringing new perspectives to the strategic debate.

The Institute's publications are designed to meet the needs of a wider audience than its own membership and are available on subscription, by mail order and in good bookshops. Further details at www.iiss.org.

All rights reserved. No part of this book may be reprinted or reproduced or utilised in any form or by any electronic, mechanical or other means, now known or hereafter invented, including photocopying and recording, or in any information storage or retrieval system, without permission in writing from the publishers.

British Library Cataloguing in Publication Data
A catalogue record for this book is available from the British Library

Library of Congress Cataloging in Publication Data

ADELPHI series
ISSN 1944-5571

ADELPHI 484–486
ISBN 978-1-032-39609-5

Contents

AUTHOR

Jonathan Stevenson is the Managing Editor of *Survival* and Senior Fellow for US Defence at the IISS. He was previously a professor of strategic studies at the US Naval War College and, from 2011–13, he served as National Security Council director for political–military affairs, Middle East and North Africa, at the White House.

ACKNOWLEDGEMENTS

I am indebted to James FitzSimonds, professor in the Strategic and Operational Research Department and director of the Halsey Alfa Group at the US Naval War College, and to William S. Murray, professor in the Strategic and Operational Research Department and director of the Halsey Bravo Group at the US Naval War College, for their invaluable insights. I must also thank Jeffrey Mazo, Benjamin Rhode and Gregory Brooks for their deft editorial assistance and the International Institute for Strategic Study's Defence and Military Analysis team for their careful technical review of the manuscript and incisive comments on it. Finally, I am grateful to the Robert and Ardis James Foundation, whose generous support made this *Adelphi* book possible.

GLOSSARY

A2/AD	anti-access and area denial
ASB	Air–Sea Battle
BCT	Brigade Combat Team
BRAC	Defense Base Realignment and Closure
CAOC	Combined Air Operations Center
CENTCOM	US Central Command
CJTF–HOA	Combined Joint Task Force–Horn of Africa
CSG	carrier strike group
EAS	European Activity Set
EFP	Enhanced Forward Presence
eNRF	enhanced NATO Response Force
EUCOM	US European Command
FAST	Marine Corps Fleet Anti-terrorism Security Team
INF Treaty	Intermediate-Range Nuclear Forces Treaty
IRBM	intermediate-range ballistic missile
IRGC	Islamic Revolutionary Guard Corps
JCPOA	Joint Comprehensive Plan of Action
LRPS	long-range precision strike
MDO	multi-domain operations
NAVCENT	US Naval Forces Central Command
NSA Bahrain	Naval Support Activity Bahrain
RAP	Readiness Action Plan
SAC	Strategic Air Command
SOF	special operations forces
SOFA	status-of-forces agreement
TLAM	*Tomahawk* land-attack missiles
UAV	uninhabited aerial vehicle
USAF	US Air Force
USMC	US Marine Corps
VJTF	Very High Readiness Joint Task Force

CHAPTER ONE

Overseas bases and US strategic posture

Since the United States became an extroverted world power during and after the Second World War, overseas military bases have been the bedrock of its nuclear and conventional deterrents and its ability to project military power and exert political influence. As of July 2021, the US operated military facilities at around 750 sites beyond its national territory.[1] While this is only about half as many as at the end of the Cold War, the number of countries hosting US bases has doubled from around 40 to 80 since that time. These bases cumulatively cost roughly US$55 billion annually – around one-twelfth of the US defence budget – to maintain and sustain.[2]

Present and future US overseas-basing arrangements merit a hard look in the light of dynamic developments in US foreign and security policy and in its military technology. There is an active debate within the US public and policy community about the desirability of reducing US global military activities and overseas presence, whether due to fatigue from fighting a 'forever war' or for more nuanced financial and strategic reasons.[3] But this desire does not necessarily translate into sound strategy. This *Adelphi* book will focus on the trade-offs between vulnerability and responsiveness and between peace-time financial savings and increased operational costs of power projection and combat deployment from reducing overseas basing. It takes into consideration the context of changing technologies and capabilities, the likely direction of US policy and grand strategy and the political and military priorities of host countries and key regional actors; it applies these benefit, risk and cost criteria to American bases in Europe, the Asia-Pacific and the Middle East in order to suggest customised basing options for each region consistent with US security.

This *Adelphi* favours a pragmatic US policy of military restraint and diplomatic emphasis. Yet some level of forward US presence is indispensable to paramount US interests and objectives. For example, active and substantial US bases in Japan and South Korea are needed to reassure these allies of the integrity of extended US deterrence vis-à-vis China and North Korea respectively, and hence to constrain Tokyo and Seoul from entertaining nuclear options of their own. Such considerations may presage more continuity than change. Washington's strategic priorities in the three primary regions – Europe, the Asia-Pacific and the Middle East – appear to allow only a marginally more modest basing posture enabled by more substantial and flexible over-the-horizon capabilities.

Some historical background
The extensive global system of US bases is relatively new. In his farewell address in 1796, George Washington, the first US president, told the American people that geography afforded them the luxury of insularity, and advised them to mini-mise engagements with other countries to preserve freedom of action: 'Why forego the advantages of so peculiar a situation? Why quit our own to stand upon foreign ground? Why, by interweaving our destiny with that of any part of Europe,

entangle our peace and prosperity in the toils of European ambition, rivalship, interest, humor or caprice? It is our true policy to steer clear of permanent alliances with any portion of the foreign world.'[4] Thomas Jefferson, the third president, was more succinct in his oft-quoted 1801 inaugural address: 'peace, commerce, and honest friendship with all nations, entangling alliances with none'.[5]

For the next hundred years or so, American governments heeded these admonitions. Most presidents saw themselves as isolationists, even if Canada, Mexico and Native American nations may have disagreed. The seminal 1823 Monroe Doctrine, which declared intervention in the Americas by extra-hemispheric powers to be potentially hostile to US interests, conversely noted that Washington would not interfere with the internal affairs of such powers or their existing colonies. The US government was called upon to project naval power in the Barbary Wars in North Africa in 1801–05 and 1815 and during the War of 1812 against Britain. But the navy was then substantially reduced, with only 42 ships and 10,000 men at the outbreak of the American Civil War in 1861, and with US naval activity notably restrained, with Commodore Matthew Perry's commercially motivated expedition to Japan in 1853–54 the singular anomaly.[6] Expeditionary ground forces were used only in the Mexican–American War in 1846–48 and to otherwise advance westward through the repression and extermination of Native Americans over the course of many decades. For most of the remainder of the century, the country's territorial expansion was confined to the North American continent, except for the government-sanctioned promotion of US influence and control in Hawaii through white businessmen, culminating in annexation in 1898. As to weighty issues of imperialism and war, the US remained tentative and pragmatic.

The US only became a distinctly proactive maritime military power beyond the Western Hemisphere with the 'Open Door Policy' under president William McKinley (1897–1901), the Spanish–American War (1898) and president Theodore 'Teddy' Roosevelt's (1901–09) 'big stick' diplomacy and support for a large, blue-water navy. In 1900, along with other great powers, the US deployed troops to Peking (now Beijing) to suppress the Boxer Rebellion. Like many expansionist powers then and now, the US justified its projection of power primarily in terms of securing access to resources and markets, so as to continue its march to economic supremacy. Washington was also becoming more assertive closer to home. In its efforts to enforce the Monroe Doctrine the US came surprisingly close to war with Britain in 1895–96 and Germany in 1902 over the involvement of these European powers in Venezuela.[7]

A brief period of enthusiasm for colonial expansion followed the Spanish–American War, which had ended with the acquisition of Guam, the Philippines and Puerto Rico from Spain. Yet the US soon returned to its traditional posture of suspicion towards direct and outright colonial rule, partly due to the brutal counter-insurgency campaign required to subjugate the Philippines. By 1904, Teddy Roosevelt remarked that he had 'about the same desire to annex [the Dominican Republic] as a gorged boa-constrictor might have to swallow a porcupine wrong-end-to'.[8]

While the US did establish permanent military outposts in Guam, the Philippines and smaller Pacific territories such as Wake Island (annexed in 1899) after the Spanish–American War, they were considered difficult if not impossible to hold in the event of war.[9] The US continued, however, to involve itself in the affairs of other states. Most notably, following Panama's separation from Colombia in 1903 in a revolution supported militarily by Washington, the US government built the Panama

Canal and heavily defended the Panama Canal Zone. Teddy Roosevelt himself brokered an end to the Russo-Japanese War in 1905. Yet Washington exercised extreme caution in committing US military power in the First World War; president Woodrow Wilson's late but vital intervention in 1917 soured the US electorate on Wilsonian internationalism in general and active out-of-area military engagement in particular.

Congress's rejection of the Versailles Treaty and the League of Nations in 1919 signalled the re-ascendance of isolationism in US foreign policy, and the Great Depression reinforced Washington's preoccupation with domestic affairs even as storm clouds gathered in Europe. American fascists and isolationists revived the elastic slogan 'America First', which had emerged as a Republican mantra in the 1880s to focus the electorate on internal industrial expansion and had even been deployed by Wilson to characterise his popular policy of US neutrality before 1917.[10] The US maintained minor Caribbean bases at Guantanamo Bay (Cuba), Puerto Rico and in the US Virgin Islands, which it had purchased from Denmark in 1917. But sea control and naval protection of America's Atlantic coast was not supported by outlying bases.

A global presence

America remained isolationist well into the Second World War. In August 1940, however, president Franklin D. Roosevelt approved a 'destroyers for bases' deal with the United Kingdom, under which London granted Washington 99-year leases on facilities in eight British territories in the North Atlantic and the Caribbean in exchange for the transfer of 50 ageing US Navy warships. After the Japanese attack on Pearl Harbor and Germany's subsequent declaration of war against the US in December 1941, America entered the conflict in both the Atlantic and Pacific theatres and accelerated the establishment of overseas US military sites. By the end of the war, these numbered over 2,000. Although many were closed when the war ended, during the Cold War the US maintained a robust network of overseas military facilities that totalled 1,600 as of 1991.[11] Post-war strategic imperatives (such as the administration of Japan and the stabilisation of the Middle East to preserve oil supplies) and Cold War exigencies of containment (such as the defence of Europe and the prosecution of the Korean and Vietnam wars) called for a more extensive overseas American conventional military presence, and the policy emphasis was on optimising a far-flung basing system rather than questioning its necessity.[12]

In Western Europe, which viewed the Soviet Union as an existential threat even before Moscow first tested an atomic weapon in 1949, US forces exceeded 250,000 personnel by 1950. Troop levels averaged 343,043 between 1950 and 1963 and stayed well above 250,000 throughout the Cold War. But in other regions deemed less central to US security, the standing American overseas military presence was considerably smaller, reflecting a generally conservative attitude towards forward presence. Leaving aside the substantial war-fighting deployments required for the Korean and Vietnam wars, and despite a number of allies and special partners in the Asia-Pacific (notably, Japan, South Korea and Taiwan) as well as a formidable strategic adversary in China, the US maintained troop levels of around 100,000 in Asia during the Cold War. In the Middle East, US forces fell from an annual average of 22,517 in 1950–63 to a low of 8,379 in 1974–80, levelling off at 12,827 in 1981–92. The substantial US accumulation of permanently deployed forces in the Middle East (initially in Saudi Arabia, later dispersed to Bahrain, Kuwait, Qatar and the United Arab Emirates) did not occur until after the First Gulf War in 1990–91. The average rose to 15,485 in 1993–2001.[13]

On balance, the US basing dispensation after the Second World War was expansive: the nuclear-armed Soviet Union quickly emerged as a monolithic rival to the West, the Cold War got under way and containment appeared to require a robust US forward presence.[14] When the Cold War ended, the resulting 'peace dividend' included a major reduction in American installations and forces overseas. Since 1988, moreover, the Defense Base Realignment and Closure (BRAC) process has periodically streamlined basing, albeit mainly within the US. In the early 1990s, Washington withdrew nearly 300,000 military personnel from foreign bases and closed or forfeited about 60% of its overseas military facilities.[15] These included major outposts such as Subic Bay Naval Base and Clark Air Base in the Philippines, Torrejón Air Base in Spain and several bases in Panama. Overall, however, the Cold War forward-base posture stayed substantially intact until the George W. Bush administration (2001–09), which undertook what it called a Global Posture Review as part of a larger effort under secretary of defense Donald Rumsfeld to transform US armed forces for a changing strategic and technological environment.[16]

The Global Posture Review specified three categories of overseas facilities: 'main operating bases', where American combat troops (and usually their families) are permanently stationed in facilities controlled and secured by the US military, such as Ramstein Air Base in Germany or Kadena Air Base on Okinawa; 'forward operating sites', housing a relatively small US support presence and used for temporary deployments or training, such as the Sembawang port facility in Singapore; and 'cooperative security locations', involving a minimal footprint and level of control, use of which is contemplated mainly for contingencies. The latter two basing types were preferred. They are less expensive, visible and vulnerable than big bases, allow more strategic and operational flexibility and stand to raise fewer political tensions. Partly because of the Global Posture Review's recommendations (and despite political, diplomatic and bureaucratic obstacles), the average number of US troops in Europe and Asia in 2002–14 had respectively fallen by around 30% and 13% compared to 1993–2001. Another factor, of course, was the need to deploy troops to Iraq and Afghanistan after the 11 September 2001 terrorist attacks by al-Qaeda: the number of troops in Asia peaked at 321,570 in 2007.[17]

The post-9/11 dispensation

After the US went to war in Afghanistan and Iraq in the wake of 9/11, America's increased military and political presence and influence abroad was sometimes described as an 'empire', with the implication that the US would do well to recognise and embrace its de facto hegemony. But most American scholars and officials were uncomfortable with this view.[18] Notwithstanding its enormous economic and political influence and periodic enthusiasm for coups via covert action and coercive regime change, historically the US has been neither inclined to run other countries nor adept at doing so.

The general US response after 2001 to the dispersed and spreading non-state threat of jihadism was a global homeland-security concept that called for pre-emptive engagement with terrorists as far from American territory as possible. This was corollary to a strategic concept prompted by 9/11 that involved exporting democracy and Western norms to ideologically and culturally inhospitable places (especially in the greater Middle East) in order to marginalise extremist elements, better harmonise local partner regimes with Western governance, and generally make the world less hostile and more receptive to the American way.[19] This vision was unmistakably primacist – and somewhat startlingly imperial, given that it called for wars to extend the trading system – and it fit the approach that

George W. Bush's administration felt compelled to adopt. Since a larger and larger economy had to be protected, the United States' forward presence needed to be expanded.[20]

Some 20 years on, the relationship between US military activity and the facilitation of global commerce now appears quite attenuated.[21] But the prescription, with respect to overseas military bases, has been substantially realised. The concept did tend to discount the pressure that local elites beholden to revisionist powers could bring to bear on bases that the US might establish in circumstances of military urgency – for example, bases in Central Asia during the war in Afghanistan.[22] The US closed its last Central Asian military base, Transit Center at Manas in Kyrgyzstan, in June 2014, mainly in response to increased geopolitical tensions with Russia over Ukraine and an anticipated US drawdown in Afghanistan.[23] But Bagram Air Base, in Afghanistan, was functionally permanent and, until the withdrawal of American forces in July 2021, continued to undergo modernisation and expansion. More compact permanent bases, such as Combined Joint Task Force–Horn of Africa (CJTF–HOA) at Camp Lemonnier in Djibouti, have been established, as well as even smaller cooperative security locations or 'lily pads' in Africa and elsewhere.

Most analysts during this period tacitly assumed the wisdom if not the inevitability of the perpetuation of the US-led liberal international order, which has since been compromised by president Donald Trump's 'America First' policy. Yet even the Trump administration (2017–21) proved unable or unwilling to tear down the structural military underpinnings of the post-9/11 version of the liberal order. Major bases in the Middle East were consolidated and expanded and maintained high operational tempo. The initial impetus for sustaining these bases (and CJTF–HOA) was the Global War on Terror, but Congress and the Pentagon appear to consider them useful, if not essential, in the new era of great-power competition.[24] Indeed, recognition of the durable US strategic interests in the region led the administration of Barack Obama to rebrand its 'pivot to Asia' (with the abrupt, zero-sum connotations of 'pivot') as a 'rebalancing', which has a gradual, fluid connotation more in line with strategic realities in the Middle East.[25]

Bring the legions home?

This ongoing strategic rebalancing from the Middle East to Asia, coupled with rising political instability in key strategic locales such as the Middle East and Eastern Europe, have made existing basing arrangements more tenuous. So has Washington's strategic retrenchment, amplified by Trump's distaste for diplomacy, including defence diplomacy. These factors have also given rise to more restrained policies with lighter US regional management roles – particularly in the Middle East – and have dampened US enthusiasm for counter-insurgency campaigns that would require large expeditionary forces and extensive regional infrastructure to support them.

Strategic inertia and substantial structural obstacles have nevertheless engendered a general preference for the status quo in terms of overseas US basing. The sweeping Goldwater–Nichols Department of Defense Reorganization Act of 1986 helped enshrine America's global basing system by establishing the unified regional combatant commands, and with them a bureaucratic inclination to maintain corresponding regional infrastructure. The value of that infrastructure appeared evident in 1990–91 and 2002–03 during the preparations to invade Iraq. Advances in military logistics, particularly via air transport, have since diminished the salience of the time element and reduced the comparative operational and tactical advantages of overseas bases, but there is still a tendency to default to the status quo. When the US Air Force (USAF) commissioned a study of forward air-base defence in 2019 in response to concerns about the increasing ballistic- and cruise-missile capabilities of potential adversaries, the authors were not asked to consider different basing options.[26]

There are, of course, sceptics who tilt towards retrenchment, arguing that a far-flung network of US bases is an outmoded relic of a forward Cold War containment strategy that facilitated flexible response to deter hegemonic Soviet adventurism.[27] In 2017, for example, then US secretary of defense James Mattis pushed Congress for a new round of the BRAC process in order to devote more resources to readiness and modernisation, attaching a report indicating that 19% of Pentagon infrastructure overall (also including domestic bases) was unnecessary.[28] But there has been no major basing-policy overhaul since the 2004 Global Posture Review. Mattis's push for a sweeping new BRAC round mostly fell on deaf ears in Congress, and the Pentagon itself declined to follow up his call for greater focus on basing efficiency after he departed in December 2018.[29] Mattis's successor, Mark Esper, concentrated instead on reviewing the efficiencies of non-military Department of Defense agencies and the individual combatant commands.[30]

But persistent budgetary constraints due to the global economic crisis, compounded by the immediate and medium-term budgetary and operational impacts of the COVID-19 pandemic, have sharpened the need for the Pentagon to scrutinise and minimise all major defence expenditures. Maintaining a base entails recurring annual fixed costs of US$50–200 million per facility, plus variable costs according to size.[31] Base consolidation, within or outside the US, would mean considerable fixed-cost savings, and relocation to the US would produce relatively high variable-cost savings. Such savings, however, would be partially offset by the costs of new construction at remaining bases to accommodate the realignment and the costs of increased rotational presence to compensate for the loss of permanent regional bases.

The trade-off between the relative vulnerability of interior and overseas bases to attack, on the one hand, and military readiness and responsiveness, on the other, is an overarching consideration in basing decisions. In 1951, for example, as part of RAND Corporation's work for the USAF, Albert Wohlstetter was asked to investigate what appeared to be the 'rather dull logistics problem' of how the Strategic Air Command's (SAC) bases could be arrayed most cost effectively.[32] He and his team concluded that the offensive military advantage provided by basing SAC's long-range bombers in forward overseas bases – close to their targets, and in line with the Cold War political consensus – was not worth their high vulnerability to a Soviet surprise attack. Although locating the strategic bomber force farther away from the Soviet Union would reduce the swiftness of a US first strike, it would decrease the force's vulnerability to a pre-emptive attack and thus facilitate an effective second strike at much lower cost.[33] The practical result was the substantial redeployment of SAC to the US interior. A seemingly banal inquiry yielded a historic strategic insight.[34] The Wohlstetter team's assessment established a sharper overall focus on the trade-off between vulnerability and responsiveness.

Forward-deployed forces can initiate action or react to an adversary's action more quickly, but they are also more exposed to hostile military action, institutional weaknesses and political sensitivities of host governments, and violent extremism (for which US personnel and facilities are attractive targets). In addition to greater responsiveness to contingencies, putative benefits of a robust overseas posture include more credible deterrence of adversaries, assurance for allies and partners and closer day-to-day engagement in diplomatic as well as military regional security cooperation. What forward US forces would specifically be required to do in terms of quick reaction, and how far forward those bases need to be, is a central issue for US basing. It is difficult to determine how far away from potential aggressors a base of operations can be to remain both safe and effective. At some ranges, a combination of passive and terminal active defences might sufficiently mitigate the threat of attack. But this could be far enough – as much as, say, 1,500 kilometres – to materially inhibit response time.

Despite the SAC decision, after the Second World War the overall superiority of the US military tilted the balance heavily in favour of forward basing. The US was able to minimise vulnerability by robustly defending and protecting its forward-based assets while securing the deterrent and war-fighting advantages of high responsiveness. Basing short-range tactical strike aircraft close to enemy targets; establishing air- and sea-domain awareness (and ultimately dominance); denying an adversary's command, control, communications, computers, intelligence, surveillance and reconnaissance; penetrating enemy air defences via stealth or suppression; and locating and destroying key targets with short-range precision-guided munitions have all been critical to the putative 'American way of war'.

In 2013, almost 60 years after its classic SAC basing study, RAND produced a nearly 500-page independent assessment of the costs and benefits of overseas-basing arrangements, keying on the trade-off between vulnerability and responsiveness. Additional subordinate factors RAND noted as relevant to basing decisions were effectiveness in protecting the US homeland from attack; the effect on proliferation, especially nuclear; the cultural impact on local and regional populations (including antagonism of potential enemies and familiarisation of potential friends); the political impact on host governments (for example, reinforcing brutal dictatorships or destabilising insurgencies); the strategic impact on nearby adversaries (for example, intensification of bilateral security dilemmas); and the effect on US bureaucratic politics (for example, inordinate encouragement of unnecessary military action due to logistical convenience).[35]

But while the RAND study was thorough and comprehensive in its coverage of US basing topics (to an extent that this *Adelphi* cannot be) it was agnostic as to the most likely and sensible US strategy going forward and light on other relevant countries' strategic outlooks. It offered little guidance, moreover, as to why the US might need specific forces forward for specific contingencies.

Evolutions in military affairs

Logistical innovations such as mobile sea-basing and expanded strategic airlift and air-throughput capacity (the volume of traffic a given facility can handle in a set time) have improved the United States' ability to deploy assets and apply combat power over long distances quickly, and new technologies are making precision strikes, long a mainstay of the US deterrent posture, possible at increasingly longer ranges. Such technologies include land-based or submarine-launched ballistic missiles or long-range bombers equipped with hypersonic glide vehicles, or even hypersonic cruise missiles.[36] Indeed, the ability to deliver conventional munitions to a target anywhere in the world quickly and precisely (known as Prompt Global Strike) has been a goal of US planners and policymakers for nearly 20 years.[37] With the 2019 termination of the Intermediate-Range Nuclear Forces (INF) Treaty, the US and Russia are free to deploy medium- and intermediate-range ground-launched missiles in Europe and Asia, which could enhance each side's prompt-strike capability while also intensifying the arms race to gain or maintain superiority.[38]

As US adversaries have developed short-, medium- and long-range precision-strike capabilities and the ability to degrade US and allied electronic and information-technology capabilities, forward bases and aircraft carriers have become significantly more vulnerable, as have enablers of rapid, long-distance deployment such as airlift and refuelling aircraft.[39] Some have even argued that the aircraft carrier's vulnerability is making it obsolete.[40] Others argue that carriers, despite warnings about their growing vulnerability, remain considerably less vulnerable than permanent overseas bases owing to their mobility.[41] Maritime and air operations conducted in real time from naval platforms such as aircraft carriers rather than from large permanent bases could strengthen deterrence, though a limited forward infrastructure would still be required to support them.[42] In any case, the US Navy would be hard-pressed to phase out such an expensive and successful platform very quickly. Similarly, sea-basing, which involves projecting power and conducting operations from vessels positioned in international waters without the need for a host nation's permission or assistance and without maintaining a large footprint ashore, does not substantially reduce the need for forward naval basing, which calls for, at a minimum, logistics support and reloading facilities.

Medium- and intermediate-range Russian and Chinese hypersonic weapons would, in particular, pose a serious anti-access and area-denial (A2/AD) threat to US forces based in Europe and the Western Pacific, respectively.[43] US (and allied) forward bases in the Indo-Pacific are at growing risk due to their relative proximity to likely threats.[44] Until recently, analysts have tended to assume that to advance US objectives, US forces would have to operate inside the range of A2/AD threats, and that this meant not only maintaining its relatively few forward bases, but also substantially hardening their defences.[45] Others have prescribed programmatic solutions, including pulling back or dispersing US bases as well as building up active and passive defences at forward bases.[46] The US military has broadly reinforced the case for less forward basing by enhancing long-range precision strike (LRPS)-based deterrence. For example, US Pacific Command has demonstrated B-1 *Lancer* bombers' ability to strike targets near Guam on missions originating from the US.[47]

Some US analysts consider maintaining a firm technological advantage in LRPS a strategic imperative, equating it with the British Empire's control of the sea at the height of its strategic pre-eminence. Just as sea control allowed the British to project power and thereby deter their adversaries at the regional level, long-range strike capabilities allow the US to overcome adversaries' A2/AD efforts and deter them at that level.[48] Until recently, the US had a significant long-range strike advantage over its rivals, but now China is ramping up its own long-range strike and air-defence capabilities and other adversaries, including Russia and Iran, are upgrading theirs as well.[49] The overall US LRPS edge has diminished.[50]

On the face of things, especially given adversaries' abilities to employ electronic warfare and impede command-and-control nodes at closer range, superior US LRPS capabilities have reduced the operational and tactical need for forward bases and enabled carriers to be deployed farther back while retaining combat effectiveness. But most long-range bombers currently in service are compelled to use stand-off weapons, and such weapons are disproportionately affected as improving enemy countermeasures increase the number of weapons needed to ensure destruction of targets. It is also harder to find, fix, track, target, engage and assess mobile targets over longer distances. This means that penetrating strike platforms – as opposed to delivery systems – are still necessary.[51] Even long-range platforms might require assistance (for refuelling, for example) from assets positioned in forward bases.[52] Furthermore, LRPS does not obviate the desirability of positioning US military personnel forward to enhance the credibility of deterrence and crisis responsiveness and to reassure allies and partners.

Rather than pulling back US strike platforms from forward areas, the Pentagon's current plans for strategic deterrence in Europe and the Indo-Pacific involve improving, dispersing and hardening them. Long-range strike capabilities – possibly including ground-based cruise, ballistic and hypersonic missiles – would be forward deployed. More capable missile defences and new space-based and terrestrial sensors and assured access to airfields, ports and other facilities would complement these capabilities. For the Indo-Pacific, for example, the plan envisages survivable, precision-strike missiles that can support air and maritime manoeuvre from distances greater than 500 km in the Western Pacific; an *Aegis Ashore* missile-defence site on Guam; a constellation of space-based radars with the ability to track fast-moving targets; a Tactical Multi-mission Over-the-horizon Radar system, capable of detecting air and surface threats, in Palau; specialised crewed aircraft to provide discrete, multi-source intelligence collection; and power projection, dispersal and training facilities in the Marshall Islands, Micronesia and Palau as well as within the US. The idea is clearly to deploy decentralised land-based systems relatively close to the Chinese mainland and other strategic areas in the Western Pacific.[53]

Impressive as they are, new technological developments in long-range strike capabilities may not radically change the central vulnerability–responsiveness calculus that governs basing considerations. The Pentagon appears poised to move from a joint military doctrine that compartmentalises military air, sea and ground operations to a doctrine of multi-domain operations (MDO) that does not. The USAF has traditionally been responsible for medium- and long-range strikes, but under MDO, as other services acquire such capabilities the task could be assigned to whichever platform is most suitable under the circumstances – from the army's 500 km-range precision-strike missile to the navy's intermediate-range Conventional Prompt Strike weapon (both currently under development) to long-range air-force capabilities.[54] This division of labour has its roots, in part, in the now-rescinded 1987 INF Treaty, which forbade the deployment of land-based ballistic and cruise missiles with ranges between 500 and 5,500 km.

The MDO doctrine contemplates a 'calibrated force posture', with most ground forces needing to be transported to the theatre of operations from bases in the continental US for a major contingency. But the continued requirement for some forward-deployed forces, the need to sustain additional troops once they are in theatre, and the premium on flexibility and multiple options are consistent with an appreciable complement of forward bases and militate against major revisions in basing.[55] The potential need to manoeuvre from strategic distances in response to threats operating from similar distances might even mean that more forces, equipment and supplies would have to be pre-positioned.[56]

The new technological operating environment could, moreover, fundamentally alter traditional assumptions about forward vulnerability versus supposed invulnerability at home. Instantaneous communications and pervasive information have increased the premium on short decision times and responsiveness. Threats that do not respect geography, such as hypersonic weapons, information warfare, pandemics, cyber attacks and climate change are increasingly salient. Widespread disease in the continental US or large-scale cyber attacks on key American targets, such as the electric grid, for example, could palpably decrease domestic resilience and quickly degrade critical national infrastructure, inhibiting or even eliminating the ability of US forces to deploy from afar.

Defending against LRPS is very difficult and expensive for US forces, insofar as they are primarily required to protect personnel and state-of-the-art military equipment. The attacking side would, in the first instance, be expending only relatively low-cost assets and thus would have the easier and cheaper task. But the generally increasing availability of hypersonic and long-range strike weapons capable of striking rear-deployed forces also reduces the relative vulnerability of forward-based ones. In terms of vulnerability, rather than simply pulling back such forces in the face of these new capabilities, it may make more sense to harden, disperse and disguise them.[57]

Advances in cyber technology cut both ways. Forward bases may be more vulnerable than more remote assets to opposing cyber activities, but forward basing also allows deployed forces greater familiarity with the regional electromagnetic environment, which is necessary to conduct effective offensive and defensive cyber operations. Other new technologies and innovations – in particular, some combination of LRPS and sea-basing – could substantially improve the United States' ability to carry out a given mission without using permanent overseas bases. But sea-basing poses formidable communications and force-protection challenges that have not yet been addressed. In the short and medium term, without convincing demonstrations, neither LRPS nor sea-basing could offset the loss in regional political traction and engagement, situational awareness and in-theatre risk reduction that withdrawal from and disinvestment in permanent bases would cause.

While new threats that render rear-base assets more vulnerable would do the same for forward bases, the vulnerability gap would close.[58] Within the next decade, conventional LRPS will reach intercontinental ranges, denying all sides sanctuary by virtue of distance alone. At that point, the notion of 'forward' basing may seem almost quaint, as all bases will effectively be forward. This weakens the case for minimising forward expo- sure of ground forces and, with the need for quicker response, tends to support the retention of overseas bases.[59] Mutual vulnerability regardless of geography could see deterrence and reassurance considerations point in the same direction.[60] China and North Korea are moving a significant proportion of their military assets underground; for the US, too, the priority is likely to be hardening, rather than redeploying, its assets.

Few opportunities, many constraints

The political circumstances of RAND's classic 1954 basing study were unusually clear and fixed. In the Cold War, most countries were strictly aligned with either the US or the Soviet Union. Wohlstetter and his team could assume that allies or partners (especially in Western Europe, where they faced an existen- tial threat) would go along with virtually any operationally defensible American policy regardless of local or regional political effects. Although France dented that confidence (and shocked the Western Alliance) in 1966 by withdrawing from NATO's integrated military command and asking that all non- French NATO troops depart French soil, the practical effect of Gallic strategic independence was operationally limited. France did not leave NATO itself, continued to participate collectively in European security decision-making and affirmed its loyalty to the Alliance during the remainder of the Cold War.[61]

Cold War strategists were methodologically pragmatic, but their strategic circumstances were tightly bounded. Basic ideas and beliefs about America's imperatives were off-limits. As stra- tegic realists, Wohlstetter and his colleagues did not question the fundamental validity of containment, which they assumed was necessary for protecting American interests, but only how best to execute the policy. They were concerned not about ends (which were taken as givens), nor about history or political nuance (which nuclear weapons were regarded as having vitiated), but about the relatedness and efficiency of intellectual processes, which they believed would yield the right result if properly framed, calibrated and orchestrated. In that sense, while RAND thinkers like Wohlstetter admired the agility of pragmatism, they were philosophically more consistent with logical positivism, which differed crucially from pragmatism in its convictions that science was value free and operated inside strict boundary conditions, that facts and values were distinct, and that scientists and ethicists ought to operate in mutually exclusive spheres. That kind of rigidity fit well with an age in which national goals and values were threatened and did not seem to need further justification, and the overriding concern was how scientifically to fulfil and consolidate them.[62]

The US now faces multiple threats and an array of complex and unpredictable crisis scenarios.[63] In the short term, the United States' qualitative edge in long-range strike capabilities and increased forward-base vulnerability to adversaries' rising precision-strike and other regional attack capabilities may afford it some opportunities to reduce its forward presence. But these advantages are tenuous.[64] It will still take longer for strike packages to travel longer distances, and the distances of air-strike assets from targets will still affect both pre-war and intra-war deterrence, and therefore crisis management. Moving US air-base locations relatively far from targets – and thus from sources of retaliation – would reduce American control over operational tempo and the range of tactical options available to US forces, and thereby limit crisis stability. As the 2013 RAND study noted, firm and consistent declaratory policies, frequent military exercises, prepositioned equipment, ongoing access to key secure facilities and confident demonstrations of long-range surge capabilities could mitigate this liability.[65] But the political reassurance that forward US bases provide to allies and partners seems to tip a delicate balance in favour of such bases. The very vulnerability of those bases puts American skin in the game, and convinces those parties that the United States' commitment to their defence is not merely theoretical insofar as a regional contingency would require the US to defend its own personnel and assets as well.

This is especially the case in areas of operations in which allies and partners perceive the US as the traditional guarantor of the status quo and are sensitive to indications of US pullback or substantial reductions in responsiveness, and in those where new threats have appeared or standing threats have intensified. The Middle East and Europe clearly qualify on both criteria. At the same time, of course, while forward basing might be necessary for sustaining alliance relationships, it is not sufficient. Basing is not a panacea or substitute for clear thinking. Local US deployments will not fully reassure their hosts if the hosts have little confidence in US strategy and policy. To be acceptable to them, for instance, a new US strategy which leverages diplomacy may have to be wedded to concrete indications of military capabilities. The Obama administration did not follow up the signing of the 2015 Iranian nuclear deal (the Joint Comprehensive Plan of Action, or JCPOA) with a discernible decrease in the US military presence in the Middle East. Broad loss of confidence in the US as an ally and partner during the Trump administration, driven home by Trump's abandonment of the Kurds in Syria in autumn 2019, also cut against a conspicuous pullback in the US forward presence in general.[66]

Contemporary geopolitics calls for pragmatism more than positivism. In today's increasingly multipolar world, in which political alignments in regions such as the Middle East and even, to an extent, the Asia-Pacific, are more in flux, US analysts do not have the luxury of assuming the validity of a standing grand strategy or the compliant strategic temperament of host countries. Nor, after Trump's disparagement of alliances and degradation of American trust and influence, can they take US primacy for granted. They need to consider local and regional circumstances more intensely. Accordingly, analysts assessing today's basing requirements must apply the probing sensitivities to trade-offs exemplified by RAND's pioneering 1954 study to political as well as operational matters.

CHAPTER TWO

Basing and US grand strategy

Historical or potential US grand strategies can be broadly analysed in terms of at least four guiding concepts: primacy or 'liberal hegemony', selective engagement, offshore balancing and isolationism.[1] Primacy implicitly rests on the conviction that the United States is singularly indispensable to international security and uniquely capable of resolving conflicts that affect regional as well as global security. This is also true, to a lesser extent, of selective engagement, under which the US intervenes only in conflicts that involve its vital national interests. Both approaches call for nimble US military responses to multiple contingencies, which a thick network of forward bases tends to facilitate. Offshore balancing, under which the US relies on regional allies and partners to settle strategic problems and will intervene militarily only as a last resort to tilt the balance in its favour, allows for a more deliberate, less time-sensitive military approach that would require a less extensive forward presence. Isolationism, in which foreign entanglements are avoided at almost any cost, would dictate a substantially smaller US overseas-basing presence.

Containment was an outward-looking grand strategy. While the lure of the 'peace dividend' after the end of the Cold War briefly looked like it might encourage an insular interlude, George H.W. Bush's notion of a 'new world order' included humanitarian intervention in Somalia, in line with a foreign policy that considered US global leadership indispensable. Embracing economic globalisation, his successor Bill Clinton pushed NATO enlargement and continued humanitarian interventions with NATO's two wars in the Balkans; when he balked in Rwanda, observers in Washington and elsewhere castigated him. Stimulated by 9/11, George W. Bush's neo-conservative foreign policy in his first term centred on the expansion of American values and influence through military intervention. The essentially primacist approach that produced the Iraq and Afghanistan military interventions was informed by a perceived need to pre-empt jihadist terrorism and to retaliate against the source of a strategic attack.

The frustrations of those engagements showed the implausibility of maximalist US policies such as sustained counter-insurgency and state-building and shifted the conversation towards offshore balancing.[2] But although Barack Obama saw the need to diminish the military dimension of US policy, he nevertheless used the military actively (if selectively) in Afghanistan, Libya, Pakistan and against the Islamic State (ISIS). Until Donald Trump, no post-war US administration had tended towards isolationism in any significant way, and under each post-Cold War president until Trump, policy was facilitated by the ready use of military assets that were easily deployable from overseas bases.

During his 2016 campaign, Trump promised to 'Make America Great Again' with an 'America First' approach and excoriated NATO allies for spending too little on defence, hearkening back atavistically to the interwar years, when many Americans felt that the Western European powers had played on Woodrow Wilson's political grandiosity and conned the US into fighting and sacrificing on Europe's behalf during the First World War. Trump also talked tough with respect to Iran and China. Overall, he raised expectations for an insular, unilateralist policy that emphasised decisive military action and minimal political–military engagement – a nebulous combination of primacy and isolationism.[3] Once in office, at least initially, he was more pragmatic than expected. He stuck to the Joint Comprehensive Plan of Action (JCPOA) and the North American Free Trade Agreement (NAFTA), criticised the expansion of Israeli settlements in the West Bank, reaffirmed the 'One China' policy, deferred to China to rein in North Korea's nuclear-weapons and missile programmes and reiterated US support for NATO.[4] In time, however, he threw caution to the wind, and within two years he had withdrawn from the JCPOA and negotiated a replacement for NAFTA. His rhetoric stoked Japanese and Korean fears that he might draw down US forces in Asia. The US withdrew troops from Syria, leaving its Kurdish allies exposed to Turkish aggression, and antagonised Iran by assassinating Qasem Soleimani, commander of the Islamic Revolutionary Guard Corps' Quds Force. An order in 2020 to redeploy 12,000 American troops from Germany raised fears among European officials that Trump might materially downgrade the US commitment to NATO in a second term that never came.[5] The uncertainty that Trump's oscillation between primacism and isolationism instilled in allies and partners, and the risk-courting opportunism it may have induced in adversaries, amplified the need to reassure the former and give pause to the latter. The administration of Trump's successor, Joe Biden, has moved quickly to repair the damage (for example, rescinding the order to withdraw troops from Germany less than a month after taking office) and American strategic priorities and postures are likely to tilt back towards the status quo ante. Biden also quickly instituted a new Global Posture Review to ensure that the US military's global footprint is optimally sized and supports US strategy.[6] The review was completed in December 2021 and its implications will be discussed in Chapter Six.

Russian and Chinese strategic innovations now challenge the American way of war in ways that will affect basing approaches. Russia, for example, has developed military capabilities such as advanced coastal defence, air-defence systems, battlefield rockets, short-range ballistic missiles and cruise missiles, and rapid-reaction forces and significant air assets in its Western Military District and Kaliningrad which, though depleted from operations in Ukraine, when replenished could complicate NATO plans to rapidly reinforce the Baltic states and Poland in a crisis. A surge-based approach (in which the US would flow forces gradually and safely to a few secure bases from which an overwhelming counter-assault would be launched) has long determined US force posture. Now, however, the logistical routes to the bases – and the bases themselves – have become vulnerable to enemy attack via long-range precision strike, anti-access and area denial (A2/AD) and other means. Elbridge Colby, a deputy assistant secretary of defense in 2017–18, has argued that the US needs forces designed to fight from the beginning of hostilities to deny an adversary such as Russia or China from achieving a fait accompli with respect to a Baltic state or Taiwan. This would require more (if smaller) and more defensible and geographically dispersed bases with more abundant pre-positioned equipment and pre-deployed forces to diminish logistical vulnerabilities and increase readiness.[7] In particular, as part of its transition to multi-domain operations, the US Army is proposing the deployment of 'relatively light' forces with a low signature that are 'capable of engaging targets in all domains at operational and even strategic ranges' as 'the linch-pin of effective joint and combined defenses' in operations in the Indo-Pacific. Such forces, says the army, 'will require dynamic posture initiatives – turn-key or warm start sites to provide opportunities for maneuver without incurring the cost and host nation imposition of traditional basing or permanence'.[8]

Thus, even the more limited US grand strategies tend to envision significant forward-deployed US forces, though with a smaller footprint; only near-isolationist policies would unequivocally dictate a comprehensively smaller overseas-basing presence. Although Trump often suggested that he would reduce US support for allies and partners in key regions, circumstances beyond Washington's control consistently militated against such a shift. These included North Korea's weapons programmes and threats; Iran's regional provocations and Saudi Arabia's aggressive reactions; Russian revanchism; and China's steadily rising military capability and regional assertiveness. This dynamic of strategically unrealistic rheto-ric from the White House in the face of regional developments that made corresponding policies all the more impracticable paradoxically ended with the need for Washington to reaffirm old commitments in order to reassure alarmed or disaffected allies and partners. Permanent forward bases are part of those commitments, even if they may no longer fully reassure US allies and partners.

Trump's actions did highlight the need to recalibrate US foreign policy, and he advanced a bipartisan consensus that the US should be more confrontational towards China as the strategic salience of the Indo-Pacific increases. The reduction of US influence and downgrading of US interests in the greater Middle East makes a degree of retrenchment there likely in the long term, calling for a policy of restraint involving lighter strategic management and operational involvement.[9] Meanwhile, a robust military presence in Europe is needed to reassure allies in the wake of Trump's uncomfortably close relationship with Moscow, his reluctance to fully embrace NATO, Russia's increasingly assertive revanchist rhetoric aimed at regaining its putative sphere of influence in Eastern Europe and the Caucasus, and of course its unprovoked and brutal aggression in Ukraine. Together these considerations suggest a more geopolitically modest – and arguably riskier – strategy that tilts towards offshore balancing. Yet in inherently unstable regions such as the Middle East and even the Indo-Pacific, offshore balancing may still require the US to maintain a large military footprint to ensure an expeditious response to sudden contingencies and to reassure allies and partners.[10] Regardless of approach, basing requirements must be determined through close analysis on a region-by-region basis.

The Middle East

In December 1978, then US national security advisor Zbigniew Brzezinski identified an 'arc of crisis' that stretched 'along the shores of the Indian Ocean, with fragile social and political structures in a region of vital importance to us threatened with fragmentation. The resulting political chaos could well be filled by elements hostile to our values and sympathetic to our adversaries.'[11] He was thinking, of course, of the Soviet Union and the potential disruption of US energy supplies from the Persian Gulf. Scarcely a year later, fearing that the Iranian revolution and Soviet intervention in Afghanistan would lead to just that, Jimmy Carter declared that 'an attempt by any outside force to gain control of the Persian Gulf region will be regarded as an assault on the vital interests of the United States of America, and such an assault will be repelled by any means necessary, including military force'.[12] This pronouncement, which would become known as the Carter Doctrine, launched the US military's geostrategic commitment to the Middle East in earnest.

At the time, the US had no major forward bases in the region. The Carter and Reagan administrations reached agreements to establish military facilities in Egypt, Oman and Saudi Arabia, and on the Indian Ocean island of Diego Garcia, a British overseas territory. The Pentagon's Central Command (CENTCOM), established in 1983, has been the most active US geographic combatant command, with an Area of Responsibility that includes Central Asia, Egypt, the Middle East and parts of South Asia. Its location in the continental US – with its headquarters at MacDill Air Force Base in Tampa, Florida – defers to regional sensitivities to a US military presence. While the collapse of the Soviet Union eliminated the original basis for the US military commitment, Saddam Hussein's 1990–91 invasion of Kuwait prompted the deployment of hundreds of thousands of American troops and substantial materiel to Saudi Arabia and nearby countries. Although Iraq was ejected from Kuwait in short order, an ongoing US forward presence was deemed necessary to enforce no-fly zones in Iraq and then to facilitate the 'dual containment' of Iraq and Iran.

Thousands of troops remained as base infrastructure was expanded in Saudi Arabia and Kuwait and extended to Bahrain (which became the Fifth Fleet's regional base), Qatar and the United Arab Emirates (UAE), mainly for air operations. After 9/11, the US invasions and occupations of Afghanistan and Iraq led to yet more US military installations in the region. Both interventions entailed protracted counter-insurgency efforts and persistent counter-terrorism operations, which made an expeditious US withdrawal difficult. The Obama administration held steady in Afghanistan but wound down the war in Iraq and refrained from intervening militarily in the Syrian civil war.

New US military involvement was limited to countering ISIS in Iraq and Syria. The Trump administration wanted to accelerate the demilitarisation of US foreign policy begun by Obama, but once ISIS was defeated, countervailing priorities, such as the administration's strategic embrace of Saudi Arabia and aggressive confrontation of Iran, interfered. While these could be considered policies in search of a strategy, they made it difficult for the US to extricate itself from the Middle East.

The region appears to be the archetypal case study of the basing challenge. Iranian attacks on US bases in Iraq both before and after the US strike on Soleimani in January 2020, and more broadly Tehran's asymmetric approach to the American forward presence in the Gulf, have turned that presence into a distinct vulnerability. It is critical to US partnerships in the region but, equally, must accommodate those partners' acute sensitivities. Meanwhile, a (perhaps temporary) fracturing of Gulf Cooperation Council unity has complicated basing arrangements.

Qatar has hosted the US Air Force's (USAF) largest Middle East contingent (including over 10,000 military personnel as well as the Combined Air Operations Center (CAOC)) at Al Udeid Air Base since 2003, after Saudi Arabia demanded an end to large-scale permanent US military presence following the Khobar Towers attack in 1996.[13] The regional headquarters of CENTCOM is also in Qatar. US relations with Doha have remained cordial despite periodic diplomatic crises, such as the suspension of diplomatic ties with and economic boycott of Qatar by Bahrain, Egypt, Saudi Arabia and the UAE from 2017–21 over Doha's support for the Muslim Brotherhood and restored diplomatic relations with Iran.

US military officials acknowledged that this dispute was hindering long-term planning at Al Udeid and, after the UAE offered Washington base access (for example, at Al Dhafra in

Abu Dhabi), indicated that the Pentagon regarded decamping to the UAE as a plausible 'Plan B'.[14] But secretary of defense James Mattis reportedly provided private assurances to Doha that the US military presence there was secure. US facilities in Qatar could not be easily replicated elsewhere. The US has invested billions in the CAOC, the most sophisticated air-operations hub ever built and the nerve centre of CENTCOM's air operations.[15] The Pentagon has appeared to presume the need to maintain Al Udeid as its main hub of US regional air operations and the Fifth Fleet facilities in Bahrain and Al Dhafra Air Base in the UAE as a third American base to support a policy of rollback against Iran.[16]

The likelihood that the United States' Middle East policy will remain in flux in the medium term and fail to lend stability to the region reinforces the operational and political importance of maintaining the present US military footprint there. And although the US has become less dependent on the Middle East for oil, the Gulf producers continue to play a central role in the global market, which the US has a strong strategic interest in securing and influencing, something the current basing structure gives it the capacity to do.[17] Russia's post-Ukraine marginalisation as an oil exporter only reinforces these interests. At the same time, given strong voices for restraint in the region, a substantially more robust regional US military posture is unlikely to take hold. On balance, strategic and operational considerations favour the status quo in terms of basing, although political circumstances could still compel a rearward reorientation.

China and the Indo-Pacific
US involvement in the Indo-Pacific in the nineteenth century focused largely on commercial interests, which US policy-makers believed did not warrant a large military presence.

After the US gained Guam, Hawaii, the Philippines and part of Samoa at the end of the century, it ostensibly appeared to be just another leading colonial power.[18] But despite evidence of Japan's hegemonic designs, the US lacked strategic cohesion in the region until the Japanese attacked Pearl Harbor on 7 December 1941. During the Second World War, Nicholas Spykman (echoed by the influential journalist Walter Lippman) argued that, to preserve the geographical advantage afforded by two ocean flanks, the US had to ensure favourable balances of power in Europe and Asia. In Asia, Washington's strategic task started with the victorious military campaign during the war and the democratisation of Japan in its aftermath, continued with the containment of Soviet-sponsored communism (by way of the Korean War), and was consolidated through a network of defensive alliances designed to secure newly decolonised states against communist subversion.[19]

A substantial and permanent military presence, anchored in air and naval bases in Japan to the northeast and in the Philippines to the southeast, endured throughout the Cold War. During the Vietnam War, US bases may have been most useful for power projection. But America's increasing economic interdependence with rising Asian economies prioritised protecting freedom of navigation and fostering overall political stability, justifying a continuing presence. According to the Pentagon's 1995 'US Security Strategy for the East Asia-Pacific Region', the goals were 'to enhance security by maintaining a strong defense capability and promoting cooperative security measures; to open foreign markets and spur global economic growth; and to promote democracy abroad' with an eye to fostering the 'constructive integration' of an economically and militarily rising China into the international community.[20] China's military and economic combativeness in the region in the twenty-first century, and

North Korea's determination to develop nuclear weapons and ballistic missiles capable of reaching the US, suggest that this strategy has not been entirely successful.

The Indo-Pacific is the most dynamic, and strategically the most important, maritime domain in the world. Some 80% of the world's goods are transported by sea, and over 60% of that trade flows through the region.[21] It is now the second-largest military-naval market (after the US) and the nature and pace of Chinese naval procurement are key drivers of strategic naval competition in the region. Beijing has the world's fastest-growing navy and New Delhi has strong aspirations to keep up. China sees itself as East Asia's natural hegemon and is increasingly assertive, while the US considers a geopolitically balanced Asia-Pacific integral to maintaining a free global commons. These circumstances (combined with diminished US stakes in the Middle East) lie behind the Obama administration's incomplete but enduring strategic rebalancing to the Asia-Pacific.

The Trump administration, for its part, shelved the terminology of rebalancing and engaged very differently in the region. It started a trade war with China and attempted to energise nuclear non-proliferation efforts with North Korea. Neither effort succeeded. North Korean leader Kim Jong-un responded to Trump's threat of 'fire and fury' in 2017 by in turn threatening 'enveloping fire around Guam', highlighting the island's vulnerability and the risks to its operational utility. Guam hosts the US military's principal regional-operational hub, including a naval base and an air base from which aircraft could be launched against North Korea. Pyongyang could be inclined to hold Guam – as US territory – hostage to American forbearance regardless of its military status, but Washington may have some incentive to relocate offensive air assets farther away or to shift to carrier-based aircraft in planning for pre-emptive or retaliatory military action.

If the North Korean nuclear threat were mitigated, whether through Chinese pressure or US diplomatic efforts, the need for a traditional forward presence could also diminish. But neither development seems likely. North Korea's rising strategic threat to the US and its allies appears persistent. In traditional US thinking, this reinforces the need for a continuing strong US forward presence in the near to medium term to deter (or potentially fight) North Korea. But Trump periodically raised the possibility of withdrawing US troops and assets from Japan and South Korea and leaving these allies to rely mainly on the US strategic nuclear deterrent and their own conventional deterrents.

In any event, Washington is compelled to plan against future Chinese efforts to push the US out of the region.[22] The US has developed a 'bifurcated' security concept, whereby Washington and Beijing are relatively cooperative at the periphery of the region but compete in what China calls the 'near seas' (the Yellow Sea, South China Sea and East China Sea) – though, judging by its advancement of its military and, in particular, its naval capabilities, and the broadly expansionist flavour of the Belt and Road Initiative, China appears intent on shrinking what it might consider its periphery, where it might be inclined to cooperate, and expanding its near seas. Geography and distance mean that US military planning and posture for the Asia-Pacific centres on naval and air operations and assets, and the operational focus on the near seas implies an ongoing need for bases in the Philippines to facilitate access.

China insists it has indisputable sovereignty over the islets and waters of the South China Sea and the concomitant right to safeguard its maritime rights. It justifies arming the naval and air bases it has established there on artificial features as a response to new US freedom-of-navigation operations and large-scale joint manoeuvres by the US and its allies, and more broadly by reference to Chinese leader Xi Jinping's vision of a global order based on a new model of major-power relations.[23] Such a construct, according to Beijing, involves three core principles: no conflict or confrontation, mutual respect and win–win cooperation. This concept is incongruent with the US determination to resist Chinese regional hegemony and challenge China in the near seas. From Washington's perspective, China's policy calls for a strengthened US alliance network, continued close-in air and maritime surveillance and an enhanced theatre-missile defence system. Furthermore, with Taiwan's increasingly independent political and cultural orientation, China's determination to reunite the island with the mainland and the likelihood of continued US–Taiwan arms deals, crises in the Taiwan Strait will become more likely.[24] China is also concerned about Washington's attempt to diversify existing alliance relationships through trilateral and multilateral arrangements (undergirded by forward bases), particularly in Southeast Asia, undermining China's efforts to bolster its bilateral defence relations in the region.

China accuses the US of taking an exclusionary approach to both its alliance network and the promotion of an outmoded global economic system. Xi has positioned himself as a saviour of global growth and champion of globalisation, rejecting the neo-liberal global economic order anchored and perpetuated by the US since the end of the Cold War, under which Washington determines the rules of the road. Instead he has put forward trilateral or multilateral structures in the spirit of 'win–win' inclusivity and a 'community of shared interests'.[25] At the same time, China has continued the militarisation of islets in the disputed South China Sea, accelerated its campaign to establish a sustained military presence in the East and South China seas, attempted to isolate Taiwan, temporised on North Korea and disrupted the unity of the Association of Southeast Asian Nations.

Given the region's global economic centrality and China's standing intention to challenge US regional military primacy, it is unlikely that any American administration would be inclined to substantially downgrade the US military's presence or activities in the region. Its military strategy stands to remain centred on maritime and long-range strike capabilities, which may leave some opportunities for reducing its ground presence in the region.

Europe and NATO

The US initially built up its military presence in Europe to fight Germany and its allies during the Second World War, but post-war demobilisation saw American military personnel levels fall dramatically. Following the creation of NATO in 1949, the US re-established and consolidated its military presence to strengthen European stability by reassuring European allies that US forces would preclude a dangerous revival of German nationalism and by deterring a Soviet invasion. By 1952, there were over a quarter of a million US military personnel stationed in Europe.[26]

Throughout the Cold War NATO functioned very effectively as a deterrent, but it conducted no military operations between 1949 and 1990. Although the Alliance's purpose seemed uncertain for a while after the end of the Cold War, it adjusted its mission in response to other contingencies and remained relevant to international security. US bases, in turn, continued to be needed to support kinetic operations. In 1990, NATO deployed early-warning aircraft and a quick-reaction force to support coalition operations in defending Saudi Arabia against Iraq. The Alliance intervened successfully in Bosnia-Herzegovina in 1995 and Kosovo in 1999 to quell ethnic cleansing and stem political discord.[27] After 9/11, NATO took on its first 'out-of-area mission', in Afghanistan, commanding the International

Security Assistance Force from 2003 through 2014. During this period, NATO also trained Iraqi security forces, undertook anti-piracy operations in the Gulf of Aden and the Indian Ocean and, over the course of seven months, intervened with airstrikes against Colonel Muammar Gadhafi's regime in Libya pursuant to UN Security Council Resolution 1973.

Russian revanchism (albeit spurred in part by NATO enlargement) also renewed NATO's purpose. Prefaced by Russia's invasion of Georgia in 2008, its 2014 invasion and annexation of Crimea refocused the Alliance – and US forces in Europe – on securing the continent against Russian depredations. Trump regularly cast doubt on NATO's value and relevance, and reportedly even planned to withdraw from the Alliance entirely.[28] But the Pentagon mitigated the impact of Trump's public comments by continuing transatlantic business more or less as usual. The wider US military community strongly believes in NATO's ongoing political value as well as its operational utility. In 2019, James Stavridis, a retired US admiral and former Supreme Allied Commander of NATO, noted that no Alliance member had ever attacked another, and that NATO had provided seven decades of peace.[29]

Despite the post-Cold War drawdown of American troops from a Cold War peak of over 400,000 to about 65,000 in 2020, the centrality of US deployments has been largely taken for granted.[30] Even so, most US bases established in Europe during the Cold War remain, and two combatant commands – US Africa Command (AFRICOM) as well as US European Command (EUCOM) – are headquartered in Stuttgart, Germany. With Stuttgart serving as a hub, the US military has used Europe as a springboard for operations in other regions, notably the Middle East. In recent years, US base closures in Europe have been driven not so much by diminished operational requirements as by more efficient base allocation under the Pentagon's

European Infrastructure Consolidation programme. For example, when the USAF announced it would pull out of UK Royal Air Force (RAF) bases in Mildenhall, Alconbury and Molesworth in 2015, it also announced it would redeploy tanker aircraft and an air special-operations group to existing bases in Germany and named RAF Lakenheath as the first permanent European base for the F-35 *Lightning* II joint strike fighter aircraft.[31] As of the end of 2021, however, none of these steps had actually been implemented; the Mildenhall relocation plan was actually cancelled in 2020 as part of the Trump administration's proposed reduction of forces in Germany.

Just after he stepped down as Supreme Allied Commander Europe and commander of EUCOM in 2016, retired USAF General Philip M. Breedlove named Russian aggression as one of the key strategic threats facing the US and the Alliance.[32] He appeared to validate concerns lodged by more hawkish observers earlier in the Obama administration that shrinking the American military presence in Europe was imprudent.[33] Russia's destabilising activities in Ukraine, annexation of Crimea, apparent revisionist intentions in the Caucasus region and strategically disruptive war against Ukraine have confirmed the point. Trump's hostility towards NATO and strategically senseless order to withdraw 12,000 US troops from Germany (seemingly as punishment for what he considered its low defence spending and coolness towards his administration) intensified calls among European officials for strategic autonomy. Yet a Europe abruptly untethered from the US would face serious risks and be more vulnerable to Russian provocations, as demonstrated by a 2019 IISS scenario-based study of European capability requirements.[34]

The US did not materially moderate its commitment to European defence during Trump's presidency, but EUCOM did undergo a fundamental change to its posture, beginning to shift from focusing on security cooperation and engagement back to defence and deterrence.[35] Contrary to Trump's assertions, too, European NATO member states have reaffirmed their 2014 pledge that those currently spending 2% of their GDP on defence would continue to do so and the others would 'aim to move towards' 2% by 2024.[36] European defence spending began increasing in 2014, before Trump was elected, due not to American hectoring but rather to heightened national threat perceptions.[37] In 2017 alone, NATO's European members increased their defence budgets by 3.6% in real terms.[38] The trend has continued, with year-on-year increases leading to a new all-time high in real terms in 2019. Despite the severe economic contraction as a result of the coronavirus pandemic in 2020, European defence spending as a percentage of GDP continued to increase steadily, from 1.21% in 2016 to 1.39% in 2019 and 1.50% in 2020.[39] This trend masks sub-regional variations; it is most marked in Eastern European states, but the number of countries increasing their share is growing. The trend of reduced personnel levels is also being reversed, but there will be no return to Cold War European troop levels, and the increases to date have not been operationally significant.[40] The 2019 IISS study indicates that, even assuming the US$357 billion price tag were to be approved, it would take 15–20 years for European militaries to make up the shortfalls occasioned by a US withdrawal from NATO.[41] While European governments' post-Ukraine mobilisation may shorten this span, the bottom line is that Europe will need ready US military assets well into the medium term.

Spending and force-level decisions should be viewed in combination with the contributions many states have also made to NATO's Readiness Action Plan (RAP), agreed at the Wales Summit in the wake of Russia's seizure of Crimea and the outbreak of armed conflict in eastern Ukraine. While

NATO (with the US) would likely win a major war with Russia, Moscow is increasingly capable of prosecuting a short conventional campaign with limited political objectives.[42] Over the past several years, NATO appears to have decided not to rely merely on fear of escalation as a deterrent, but also to degrade Russia's ability to gain local advantages within NATO and thus shift the political and military burden of escalation back onto Moscow.[43] The RAP was designed to reassure NATO's Eastern European member states and enable the Alliance to better respond to current security challenges in the region, including those emanating from the south. Among other measures, larger and more complex exercises were to be held, and a Very High Readiness Joint Task Force (VJTF) was established to act as the spearhead for the NATO Response Force, which was itself to increase in strength from 13,000 to 40,000.

At the 2016 Alliance summit in Warsaw, NATO Secretary General Jens Stoltenberg announced that the RAP had been fully implemented, but it was agreed that more was required. After the Wales Summit, NATO Force Integration Units were set up in eight East European states to act as liaisons between NATO armed forces and host national armed forces, and to assist the rapid deployment of NATO forces including the VJTF. Each comprised about 20 host-nation and 20 NATO personnel. These were now given an additional coordinative task, after NATO agreed to deploy four multinational battalion-strength battlegroups in Estonia, Latvia, Lithuania and Poland as part of an 'Enhanced Forward Presence' (EFP), intended to boost deterrence and defence on NATO's eastern flank. Even the improved deployment time afforded by these steps might not be quick enough in a Baltic scenario such as that explored by the IISS study. Nevertheless, host nations welcomed the EFP deployments as a significant reassurance measure, and all of them are now operational.[44] NATO's

Brilliant Jump II exercise (28 October–6 November 2020) successfully tested its ability to deploy the VJTF from home stations in the Czech Republic, Poland and Spain to Lithuania, and to integrate it with the EFP based there.[45]

In addressing possible contingencies in the Baltic states in particular, NATO members' armed forces (many of which were reshaped to engage in crisis-management and out-of-area operations) are required not only to rediscover faded skills and refresh reduced capabilities, but also to be prepared to conduct opposed-entry operations in a contested battlespace and to suffer significant casualties. Yet they cannot abandon the post-9/11 mission set, which includes combatting human trafficking and piracy, as well as counter-terrorism. Tackling these missions simultaneously requires adaptable and innovative national armed forces, as well as a more flexible NATO with agile command structures. At least in the medium term, the lion's share of operational responsibility will continue to fall on the US, which will be required to provide most capabilities and to take the lead in solidifying NATO's conventional deterrence in light of a more aggressive and unpredictable Russia, especially against the background of the 2021–22 Ukraine crisis and war.

In particular, NATO will require a robust but controlled area-access strategy to reinforce its EFP forces with larger conventional ground-force units.[46] Forces from allies such as Denmark, the United Kingdom and the US (among others), smoothly deployable on a bilateral basis outside of NATO's multilateral command structure, would be required to bolster the extant VJTF and the 'second wave' Enhanced NATO Response Force (eNRF). This would necessitate more aircraft which are able to mobilise quickly and operate in heavily defended areas covered by A2/AD measures. US assets would be critical to the rear-echelon joint and combined air and naval support needed for area access in a major contingency.[47] Key components include ground forces, land-based air-combat assets and strategic logistical capabilities.[48] The US basing presence in Europe will thus have to increase for NATO to move from deterrence by virtue of its historical reputation to a more reliable and confident deterrence by actual preparedness. Inasmuch as the strength of NATO's deterrent ultimately lies in the strength of the Alliance itself, there are also political motives for an increased presence.

The US undertook the expansion of its overseas bases during the Cold War largely as part of a tripwire strategy, which alleviated the fears of crucial allies hosting the bases that they could not depend on the US deterrent. Of course, the US did end up fighting serious and costly hot wars in Korea and Vietnam. But the bases have borne out their anticipated utility, however anachronistically, in projecting American power. Maintaining them, to be sure, has increased both strategic and operational costs to the US. Strategic costs include intensified security dilemmas vis-à-vis strategic adversaries like China, Iran and Russia, encouraging them to spend more on their militaries and provoke the US; implicit support for undemocratic and abusive regimes; enhanced perceptions of the US as a militaristic and imperialistic nation uninterested in diplomacy and the peaceful resolution of conflict; and negative publicity in host countries and elsewhere due to crimes committed by US personnel, as in Okinawa and South Korea.[49] Operational costs include more potent inducements to terrorist recruitment and increased forward vulnerability to terrorism – demonstrated by Saudi Hizbullah's 1996 bombing of the Khobar Towers military-housing complex in Saudi Arabia – and to the military power of adversary nations.[50] Nevertheless, the reality of great-power rivalry, its global sweep, the improbability that the US would respond with an insular or timid grand strategy, and the operational requirements of implementing an energetic one counsel more continuity than change in US overseas basing.

CHAPTER THREE

Optimising US regional footprints: the Middle East

As of November 2021, the United States had some 36,500 military personnel deployed in the greater Middle East, with the bulk in Qatar (10,000), Kuwait (10,000), the United Arab Emirates (UAE) (5,000) and Bahrain (4,700).[1] Qatar has hosted the US Air Force's (USAF) largest Middle East contingent (including over 10,000 military personnel) as well as the Combined Air Operations Center (CAOC) at Al Udeid Air Base for almost 20 years. The regional headquarters of the Pentagon's Central Command (CENTCOM) and CENTCOM'S naval component (NAVCENT) are also in Qatar. Naval Support Activity Bahrain (NSA Bahrain) is the headquarters of the US Fifth Fleet, which operates in the Persian Gulf, the Gulf of Oman and the Arabian Sea. The USAF's 380th Air Expeditionary Wing operates from the UAE's Al Dhafra Air Base, while the contingent in Kuwait comprises mostly US Army troops and pre-positioned equipment.

Like Barack Obama and Donald Trump, Joe Biden would like to reduce the US footprint in the Middle East.[2] But durable US strategic interests and rising instability in the greater Middle East call for the continuation of a substantial US military presence in the short to medium term. The continued presence in Bahrain, and the expanded presence in Saudi Arabia, are largely contingent on Iranian threats; if the US and Iran are unable to reach a new deal on the latter's nuclear programme and perhaps other security matters, there may be little immediate scope to reduce US strength in those countries, despite Biden's decision to end US support for Saudi Arabia's war against the Houthi rebels in Yemen. The size of the residual US force in Kuwait is likewise largely dependent on operations in Iraq, where the ongoing threat of the Islamic State (ISIS) makes it difficult to substantially redeploy that force.

Preventing Iran from gaining nuclear weapons or substantially increasing its regional influence, containing or defeating potentially resurgent jihadist groups such as ISIS or al-Qaeda, and ensuring preparedness for a range of other contingencies affecting international security remain essential US political–military goals. Although the need to service strategic priorities elsewhere, and a relative decline in US influence in the region, mean that Washington is likely to continue to pull back in the greater Middle East and will need to concentrate selectively on forging regional stability, the US is nevertheless still compelled to protect strategic interests in the region when they are threatened. The Pentagon apparently assumes it needs to maintain Al Udeid as its main hub of US regional air operations and the Fifth Fleet facilities in Bahrain and Al Dhafra Air Base as a third American base to support a policy of rollback against Iran.[3]

Contingencies

The possibility that the US may significantly ramp up kinetic military activity in the Middle East, while relatively remote, is nevertheless real. The range of contingencies potentially calling for a military response includes an Iranian breach of a renewed nuclear deal (especially an outright sprint for a nuclear weapon); an Iranian attempt to close the Strait of Hormuz and block international trade (in particular, oil shipments); increased Iranian attacks on US bases; an attempt by a resurgent ISIS to retake territory in Syria and Iraq or to invade Jordan; a threatened or actual terrorist or insurgent attack on US diplomatic personnel; rising jihadist control of Libya's government and assets; and increased pirate activity in the Gulf of Aden and the Indian Ocean. This is a broader range of contingencies than applies to any other area of US operations.

Iranian provocations

Resumption and acceleration of Iranian nuclear-weapons activity could prompt Washington to intensify and refine contingency planning for pre-emptive military action and to deploy additional US military assets to the region to show resolve, firm up the US extended-deterrence posture and to prepare for military action to prevent Tehran deploying a nuclear weapon or achieving a breakout capability. The most effective ordnance for airstrikes against Iranian nuclear sites, such as 14-tonne bunker-busting bombs, would require land-based aircraft operating out of regional bases (such as those in Diego Garcia, Kuwait, Qatar, UAE or Saudi Arabia) rather than carrier-based planes.[4] To minimise the danger of Iranian retaliation, however, the US might decide to strike a range of additional targets, including medium-range ballistic-missile sites, cruise-missile sites, airfields, naval assets, chemical plants and oil refineries. Carrier-based aircraft as well as cruise missiles launched from surface ships or submarines could be used for such operations. The US could also elect to pressure Iran without actually attacking its military facilities, but rather targeting oil refineries and other economic targets. A naval blockade of Iranian exports would be another option, though it would likely provoke swarm attacks that could tax and eventually penetrate American defences.[5]

While increasing energy independence has afforded the US greater discretion in its Middle East strategy than it once enjoyed, the substantial exclusion of Russian oil exports from world markets in the wake of the Ukrainian–Russian war has, to an extent, restored Gulf oil producers' market power and strategic importance. In any case, they will keep determining the world price, US companies will continue to have a stake in their wells, and the Strait of Hormuz, through which nearly one-fifth of the world's oil supply passes, will remain a major chokepoint. Iran has developed a capable navy that could temporarily close the strait (or the Bab el-Mandeb Strait, which accounts for about 5% of global oil trade) using mines, and impede US countermeasures with small fast-attack boats, anti-ship cruise or ballistic missiles, and air defences.[6] The Islamic Revolutionary Guard Corps' (IRGC) *Great Prophet 9* naval exercise in February 2015 in the Strait of Hormuz, which involved a mock attack on a US aircraft carrier by missiles and small boats, appeared to be a public declaration of Iranian intent to assert its regional maritime capability.[7] Iran's subsequent conduct has only confirmed this.

A US military response to Iranian provocations in the Strait of Hormuz would probably involve the coordinated employment of minesweeping capabilities (possibly including the Royal Navy, as US capabilities are relatively limited in this area), anti-ship cruise missiles and air defences. The US Navy would need at the very least a carrier strike group (CSG), other surface vessels and land-based offensive airstrike capabilities targeting Iranian missile sites ashore to conduct maritime-security operations and to engage in more kinetic operations if necessary. The potential for escalation and a protracted engagement would be high.[8] US Navy ships also need to be on call to escort merchant ships through the strait to deter Iranian harassment or even major military action, though it is possible that regional maritime combined task forces – in which the US has long participated – could be used for this purpose and reduce the demand for US forces.[9]

Likewise, in an elevated contingency in Yemen, the US would likely deploy several warships from a CSG – potentially including a carrier, guided-missile cruisers, destroyers, minesweepers and amphibious assault ships – to conduct maritime-security operations in the Gulf of Aden and the Arabian Sea. These would include teams capable of intercepting, boarding and searching vessels suspected of carrying arms and of reinforcing the UN-imposed arms embargo and blockade led by Saudi Arabia. In April 2015, for example, the US mobilised nine ships in response to increased Iranian naval activity near Yemen.[10] In late 2020, the navy dispatched a guided-missile submarine and two guided-missile cruisers through the Strait of Hormuz, apparently in response to rocket strikes by Iranian-backed militias in Iraq.[11]

Syria

The Syrian civil war has drawn in Iran, Hizbullah and Russia on the side of the Bashar al-Assad regime, and Qatar, Saudi Arabia, the UAE and (less extensively) the US on the opposition side. Deepened US involvement in Syria, whether for strategic or humanitarian reasons, would be unlikely to entail any large-scale US ground deployment, but many contingencies might require ramped-up air and maritime assets and operations.

A substantial worsening of the refugee crisis, for example, could amplify calls for no-fly zones, humanitarian corridors and safe havens to secure the provision of aid by the United Nations and other non-governmental organisations within Syria, and for Washington to help stage the transfer and ensure the safe flow of food and medicine to border areas in neighbouring states, especially Jordan and Turkey.[12] This would typically involve both land- and carrier-based aircraft, and would significantly increase the tempo of land- and carrier-based air operations in the CENTCOM area of responsibility.[13]

US action to deter indiscriminate regime attacks would likewise leverage maritime assets. When US and allied intelligence concluded that the regime had used chemical weapons in a large-scale attack in August 2013, killing almost 1,500 people, the planned response involved limited precision strikes by *Tomahawk* land attack missiles (TLAMs) launched from guided-missile destroyers or attack submarines. Although last-minute diplomacy forestalled military operations, five such destroyers and a few attack submarines were deployed to the region and prepared to launch strikes.[14] In response to Syrian chemical-weapons use in April 2017, the US employed 59 TLAMs launched from two destroyers in the Mediterranean Sea, and again in 2018 employed 19 Joint Air-to-Surface Standoff Missiles (JASSMs) fired from bombers flying out of Al Udeid supported by fighter, tanker and electronic-warfare aircraft also based at Al Udeid, as well as 66 TLAMs: 30 from the cruiser USS *Monterey*, 30 from the destroyers USS *Laboon* and USS *Higgins* and six from the submarine USS *John Warner*.[15]

Other contingencies

Other important contingencies would require fewer assets. Rising jihadist control of Libya's government and Libyan assets could also provoke a US military response, but this would likely be highly selective and tactical, with an eye towards helping moderate government forces re-establish control. Such an effort would probably involve TLAMs fired from naval platforms, combat aircraft out of Aviano Air Base in northeastern Italy staged through Naval Air Station Sigonella in Sicily, or perhaps US special operations forces (SOFs). There is some precedent: in summer 2013, armed separatist militias blockaded three of

Libya's main oil ports in Cyrenaica, deprived the central govern-ment of much-needed revenues while demanding a greater share of the country's oil wealth and brought the government to the point of collapse. In March 2014, at the Libyan govern-ment's request, US Navy SEALs took possession of the tanker *Morning Glory*, which was carrying 234,000 barrels of oil illegally exported from Libya's El Sider port a week earlier. The recovery of the oil (in international waters) was intended to show the militias in the eastern provinces that the government was not powerless to thwart them, and thus to function as a deterrent.[16] In 2016 the US also carried out strikes against ISIS in Libya supported by aircraft from Naval Air Station Sigonella in Sicily, as well as drones launched from ships, a base in Jordan and a newly established secret base in Tunisia. The fact that Naval Air Station Sigonella is a US European Command asset while the Jordan base was under CENTCOM raised logistical concerns, prompting the Pentagon to establish the Tunisian base.[17]

Jordan, one of Washington's closest Arab partners, legiti-mately fears an ISIS insurgency, albeit less so since ISIS's defeat and loss of territory in Iraq and Syria. The US Army maintains Area Support Group–Jordan (which has become a more impor-tant regional hub by virtue of taking on supplies from three closed US bases in Qatar) to support contingency operations and military-to-military engagement with the host nation.[18] US equipment deployed in Jordan includes a squadron of F-16C *Fighting Falcon*s and a squadron of MQ-9A *Reaper* drones. Although the US would not deploy additional ground troops in substantial numbers to assist Amman to repel ISIS, it would probably provide robust material and intelligence support, SOF for training and advice and, should Jordanian forces come under substantial pressure, air support.[19]

A terrorist or insurgent attack on US diplomatic personnel is most likely in the Middle East, and the US is highly sensitised to this possibility due to the September 2012 jihadist attack in Benghazi, Libya, in which US Ambassador Chris Stevens and three other Americans died. In the event of elevated threats to the safety of US diplomatic and civilian support personnel in the region, Marine Corps Fleet Anti-terrorism Security Teams (FASTs) – comprising roughly 50 marines – could deploy to bolster the standing Marine Security Guard and the State Department's Regional Security Officers, to secure embassy compounds or military bases, train local security forces and evacuate US personnel. In recent years FAST platoons have been dispatched to Egypt, Iraq, Libya and Yemen. Such teams could be sent from NSA Bahrain or Naval Air Station Rota in Spain, using MV-22 *Ospreys* refuelled (should they need to loiter for an evacuation) by KC-130 *Hercules* tanker aircraft and protected by a range of combat aircraft, some based on navy surface ships.[20]

Since 2012, NSA Bahrain has hosted Combined Task Force 151 (CTF-151), a multinational force which conducts sea and air maritime-security patrols and other operations in the Gulf of Aden in coordination with the European Union's *Operation Atalanta* and partner forces under national command. Such international naval efforts have kept a lid on pirate activity in the Gulf of Aden and the Indian Ocean in recent years, but an increase in activity could dictate a commensurate uptick in CTF-151 operations and US Navy participation therein.

Basing implications

In recent years, Al Udeid Air Base in Qatar and NSA Bahrain have become less politically secure. US facilities in Qatar could not be easily replicated elsewhere, and the CAOC at Al Udeid is crucial to ongoing US air operations in the region.[21] Al Udeid appears to be the least expendable US forward base in the region. The Qatari leadership, however, likely feels protected by US dependence on Doha for its ability to wage war in the region. Doha has proceeded, largely unperturbed, with an independent foreign and security policy, and US air operations based in Qatar have continued unimpeded even during regional diplomatic crises. Under Trump, the US and Saudi Arabia did pursue a strong bilateral strategic alignment, and in June 2019 CENTCOM began deploying US aircraft, personnel and *Patriot* missile-defence systems to Prince Sultan Air Base in order to counter Iran's threat to Saudi Arabia.[22] But Riyadh would probably balk at resuming a role as host of US forces on a permanent basis, for the same reasons it asked the US to exit after the Khobar bombing in 1996.

The viability of NSA Bahrain is more tenuous. In 2010, the US Navy began a five-year, US$580 million programme to double the base's area, add several new utility buildings and expand port capacity with a new harbour-patrol facility and small-craft basin.[23] This has increased Washington's incentive to keep the navy in Bahrain, just as heavy investment has solidified the US basing commitment in Qatar. Furthermore, the conventional wisdom is that Bahrain's proximity to the Strait of Hormuz palpably strengthens US deterrence vis-à-vis Iran and facilitates US maritime policing of the area and safe passage for international maritime traffic.[24]

Bahrain's domestic political situation puts its US bases on far less secure footing than those in Qatar. Doha's equitable treatment of its minority Shia population, relative neutrality towards Iran and high per capita wealth, owing to easy-to-extract natural-gas reserves, insulate it to some extent against internal political dissent. By contrast, Sunni-dominated Bahrain has a history of repressing its Shia majority, has a high fiscal deficit due to the downturn in oil prices, is closely supported by and aligned with Saudi Arabia and is hostile to Iran. It is thus structurally susceptible to political instability.

In 1981 Shia militants operating as the Islamic Front for the Liberation of Bahrain staged a failed coup with Iranian backing, and in the 1990s conducted a campaign of bomb attacks on soft civilian targets. More broadly, from 1994 to 1999 a coalition of leftists, liberals and Islamists engaged in an 'uprising of dignity', seeking democratic reforms with significant international support.

Dissent abated when Emir Hamad bin Isa Al Khalifa established a constitutional monarchy in 2002. His reformist National Action Charter was approved by 98.4% of Bahraini voters. In 2011–13, however, the Arab Spring revived Shia desires for political equality and freedom. Violent Shia protests in Bahrain, encouraged by Iran, prompted a brutal crackdown by the monarchy and revealed a considerable degree of political risk. In the wake of government detentions, torture, brutality and censorship, Shi'ites have remained agitated and restless. In May 2015, the US House of Representatives passed an annual defence bill requiring the Pentagon to make plans for relocating the US naval base should political reforms not occur in Bahrain. In response, the Bahraini government indicated that it did not consider domestic political matters relevant to its strategic relationship with the US.[25] The provision was not included in the final enacted version of the bill.

More recently, the Abraham Accords, whereby Israel established normalised relations with the UAE and Bahrain, appear to have eased worries about US basing in Bahrain while refocusing attention on deterring Iran, thus reinforcing the status quo. In November 2021, Israel joined Bahraini, Emirati and US naval forces for the first time in combined maritime-security exercises in the region.[26] Nevertheless, improved relations with Israel have little to do with Bahrain's internal political problems, so the US seems compelled to consider the possible loss of the Bahrain base, whether due to the fall of the Bahraini monarchy or the political infeasibility of continued US support for it. In the past, the US has sometimes looked the other way when confronted with its Middle Eastern hosts' illiberal domestic politics, but it may be less inclined to do so in the wake of the assassination of Saudi journalist Jamal Khashoggi and in light of standing strategic pressures to draw down in the region.

There is, to be sure, no ready regional alternative to the base in Bahrain. Other port facilities do exist, but they are suboptimal. The New Port Project in Qatar would meet technical and logistical requirements, but the recent and potentially enduring tensions between Qatar and Saudi Arabia militate against increasing US reliance on the former. Shuaiba port in Kuwait is well located and could accommodate US ships. Kuwait has a strong and long-standing relationship with the US, and a status-of-forces agreement (SOFA) in place. But political instability and illiberality (albeit lacking the pointedly sectarian character of Bahrain's) could raise similar problems. Bases in Kuwait are, moreover, within range of a number of Iranian missiles. The UAE commercial port of Jebel Ali is the only other regional alternative that can support US Navy deep-draft vessels, but there is no existing SOFA between the US and the UAE, and the US Navy in any case would not enjoy exclusive access, a highly desirable if not strictly necessary perquisite, especially during conflict.[27]

Outside the Persian Gulf, Diego Garcia, the port of Fujairah in the UAE and the port of Duqm in Oman are additional possibilities.[28] Diego Garcia is oriented towards land-based air-force and navy air operations in Southwest Asia and is too far from the Gulf to provide useful regional support to a CSG. The legal status of the US base (leased from the United Kingdom in 1966) is also shaky, as Mauritius, a former British colony that has enjoyed sovereignty over most of the atoll since decolonisation, has been pursuing international legal challenges to the

UK's retention of sovereignty over the small portion housing the US base.[29] Oman has granted the US access to military facilities since 1980 and the US Navy has shown interest in turning Duqm into a logistics and maintenance hub precisely because of its distance from contested waters.[30] The Royal Navy already has a logistics hub there, having overhauled a frigate in Duqm in 2020–21.[31] Its port infrastructure has been enhanced in recent years and a US CSG stopped there in April 2021 for a sustainment and logistics visit.[32] But utilising these relatively remote locales would be risky as it would necessitate accessing the Gulf through the Strait of Hormuz during a crisis. Muscat is also likely to harbour some worries that permanently hosting a large American force would compromise its customary mediatory and quasi-neutral role in regional affairs.[33]

Home-basing – locating the forces now in Bahrain stateside – does not appear feasible either. While US naval forces currently headquartered in Manama could be brought home – CENTCOM itself is headquartered in Tampa, Florida, and the US recently demonstrated that it could run Middle East air operations out of the continental US (Shaw Air Force Base instead of Al Udeid) – the physical absence of US forces would decrease US political influence.[34,35] Indeed, the US withdrawal from Iraq and Afghanistan, its restraint with respect to Syria and its disinclination to engage Iran militarily have only deepened worries among regional allies that the US is pulling out of the Middle East. More concretely, if a persistent US carrier-group presence in the region is essential (see below), home-basing is not an option. Carriers and their supporting ships require maintenance, and, with respect to the Middle East, home-basing would dictate an excessively long response time to a contingency.

The only theoretical alternative to a forward base to replace NSA Bahrain, then, would be sea-basing. Sea bases can dispatch helicopters behind enemy lines, overwhelm enemy surface ships with small boats and conduct clandestine rescue missions. They can also serve as seaports, floating hospitals, logistics warehouses and specific launching bases for relatively small-scale expeditionary attacks. They broadly advance the goal of multi-domain operations of decreasing dependence on fixed sites that are easier to target.[36] And they have proven useful in counter-piracy, maritime security, humanitarian aid, disaster relief and some crisis-response operations.[37] But sea-basing poses considerable operational problems for larger-scale, highly kinetic undertakings. Sustaining and operating a combat-ready fleet requires extensive support and intensive maintenance, which, supplied by the US logistics resources deployed in Bahrain, cannot be safely, comfortably or reliably provided in theatre without a permanent naval base. An amphibious command ship, for example, holds only about 930 people – less than a fifth of the 5,000 service members stationed in Bahrain.[38]

Bahrain and other Gulf Arab countries could, moreover, construe moving the Fifth Fleet and NAVCENT headquarters to a sea base as a harbinger of broader US withdrawal from the region, which would reduce US leverage for facilitating the very political reform whose absence the pullback from Bahrain was intended to protest; embolden extremists on both sides; produce further instability and suppression; and make reform even less likely. Even as matters stand, the Shia opposition regards the US presence as exerting a moderating influence on the Bahraini government.[39]

CENTCOM's area of operations will not always, or even usually, constitute a permissive environment appropriate for sea-basing under current capabilities, and quick-reaction requirements make home-basing infeasible. This implies that maintaining a protected port facility within the confines of the

Persian Gulf is essential, especially given the vulnerability of ships transiting the Strait of Hormuz to mines, anti-ship cruise missiles and small-boat attacks – all demonstrated Iranian capabilities.[40] Bahrain remains the best of several problematic alternatives. It is possible that sea-basing options will become more viable in the long term. But, as with Al Udeid in Qatar, the US appears to have little choice but to keep NSA Bahrain intact while maintaining a fine diplomatic balance with the monarchy.

Carrier relevance

Whether a persistent US CSG in the region is operationally indispensable, as some argue, is open to question. The US Navy has had gaps in carrier operations in CENTCOM on several occasions in recent years, and US forces have frequently under-taken major strike operations in the region without any carrier involvement. But US forces may need to respond swiftly and heavily in some cases, and carriers provide the most robust capa-bilities to do so. In certain contingencies, such as an impending Iranian breakout to nuclear capability, the US would almost certainly need to deploy two carrier groups to the region to execute preventive action. Beyond their ability to react quickly, carriers represent immediately accessible American power and capability without the prior use of force while also strength-ening American deterrence. Conversely, their absence could tempt adversaries to engage in destabilising activities. It was the dispatch of the USS *Theodore* Roosevelt in April 2015, for example, that induced nine Iranian merchant ships, escorted by IRGC gunships and probably running guns to the Houthis in Yemen, to return to port.[41]

Carriers allow the US to conduct sustained air-combat operations without having to rely entirely on the cooperation or facilities of allies or partners. A decision to use force in the Middle East is difficult enough without the additional hurdle of coordinating operations with allies (however friendly) on a case-by-case basis.[42] In practice, the US has managed both. During the early stages of the US air campaign against ISIS in 2014, delayed approval by host nations held up the participation of land-based aircraft. An initial B-1 *Lancer* strike mission was curtailed over concerns about Qatari clearance, but the plane was able to hand its targets to navy F/A-18s. Air force F-15E and F-16C aircraft based in Jordan and the UAE were executing strike missions the following day, as were MQ-9 *Reaper* drones deployed out of Iraq and Kuwait.[43]

The US does face an ongoing problem of carrier overstretch. In late 2015, only five of America's ten carriers were operational; the remainder were undergoing or preparing for 'deep maintenance'. From autumn to early winter in 2015–16, for the first time since 2007 the US had no carrier presence in the Persian Gulf or the Arabian Sea.[44] Potential contingencies loomed, with instability in Iraq, Libya, Syria and Yemen and with Russia having militarily insinuated itself into Syria. But the carrier gap did not leave the US without a regionally based tactical air capability. Filling that need were land-based USAF fighter and bomber aircraft operating out of Jordan, Kuwait, Qatar and the UAE. Although they did not constitute a direct replacement for a carrier – they were deployed in the region anyway – in terms of raw numbers and combat capability, these assets exceeded the contribution of just one carrier air wing. Also available were AV-8B *Harrier* IIs, attack and assault support helicopters and MV-22 *Ospreys* operating from amphibious assault ships and other vessels in Amphibious Readiness Groups and allied carriers such as France's aircraft carrier *Charles de Gaulle*.[45]

Extended deployments by carriers over the past several years – averaging 6.4 months from 2008–11 and increasing to over 8.2 months from 2012–15 – have stretched the period required for inter-deployment maintenance from 14 months to, in some cases, 23 months.[46] The commissioning of the USS *Gerald R. Ford* in July 2017, which gave the US the eleventh carrier it had lacked since the USS *Enterprise* was deactivated in 2012, will ameliorate this problem to some degree when it deploys in 2022.[47] But with the rebalancing to the Asia-Pacific, where security is maritime-centric, and with Russia stepping up its naval challenge to the US in both Europe and the Pacific, the operational pressure on the US carrier fleet will continue unabated, if not increase.[48] The Pentagon should endeavour to close the gaps in carrier coverage systematically rather than piecemeal or episodically. One possibility would be to procure a twelfth aircraft carrier, but that is unlikely in the near to medium term due to financial and bureaucratic pressures.[49] The US is already planning to replace nine of the ten current *Nimitz*-class carriers with *Gerald R. Ford*-class vessels by 2058; the namesake is already operational and a second has been launched but not yet commissioned.

A second possibility would be to develop maintenance facilities within the region but outside the Persian Gulf.[50] A prime site, as noted above, would be Duqm, which US Navy ships have used for limited maintenance for years. In April 2017, an Omani–British joint venture opened the Duqm Naval Dockyard specifically to provide maintenance and support to naval ships.[51] The US Navy has already recognised the new facility as enhancing its ability to operate forward at task-group level, and noted that 'the port of Duqm provides a unique capability to support repairs and maintenance which would otherwise need to be completed in homeport'.[52] While a 1980 facilities-access agreement allows the US to use Omani air bases, it does not have any bases of its own in the country, and its only regular presence is a small US Air Force support contingent that manages fuel storage. The 2019 Strategic Framework Agreement affords the US similar access rights to ports.[53]

Changing environment

The regional operations that American bases, ships and aircraft currently undertake are essentially the same as those they have undertaken over the past two decades, but their exposure to hazards has changed significantly as modern weapons technology has diffused from the West to countries such as China, Iran, North Korea and Russia. In the Middle East in particular, improving Iranian ballistic-missile capabilities are increasing the risk to forward-deployed US forces. In June 2017, for example, Iran apparently launched six *Zolfagar* short-range ballistic missiles at ISIS-related targets in Iraq, some 650 kilometres distant, and filmed at least some of the impacts from an uninhabited aerial vehicle (UAV) circling above the targets.[54] This demonstrated that the *Zolfagar* would have the range to strike airbases in Qatar and the UAE. The operationalisation of UAVs for damage assessment, including outfitting them with infrared cameras, was not a trivial accomplishment, and suggested that Iran was improving its ability to strike – with reasonable precision – targets in neighbouring countries, including forward-deployed US forces. The drone and cruise-missile attack on Saudi oil infrastructure in September 2019 and ballistic-missile strikes on US bases in Iraq in January 2020 in retaliation for the attack on Qasem Soleimani confirmed this development. Iran also conducted a ballistic-missile exercise targeting a mock aircraft carrier in 2020, and in 2021 conducted another that saw missiles impact the sea within 160 km of a US carrier, but practically speaking, American CSGs are not especially vulnerable to such attacks.[55]

Other things being equal, redeploying substantial US forces out of the region to avoid such vulnerability would degrade America's regional deterrent by increasing the time it would take to retaliate for an attack. The only obvious way to allow redeployment while preserving a reliable deterrent would be to shift US declaratory policy on retaliatory response from promptness to assuredness. But the latter would still depend on access to the region and could require the construction of airbases beyond the future effective range of Iranian missiles, increased reliance on seaborne forces, the threat of military invasion or even the threat of a nuclear strike. These options all have negative financial, political or doctrinal aspects that make them less appealing than the status quo, even though this is increasingly brittle.

CHAPTER FOUR

Optimising US regional footprints: China and the Indo-Pacific

Washington's relative rebalancing to the Asia-Pacific does not exempt the region from America's overall strategic retrenchment, with its more restrained policies, lighter US regional-management roles and dampened US enthusiasm for counter-insurgency campaigns that require large expeditionary forces and extensive regional infrastructure to support them. Future armed conflict in the region is likely to be heavily weighted towards naval and air engagements and not involve counter-insurgency or large ground deployments. But the trade-off between vulnerability and responsiveness in basing considerations applies to even these limited tasks, and it is particularly acute in the Indo-Pacific.

Since the primary American interests in the region are freedom of navigation, the facilitation of global trade and the protection of regional allies, it is politically difficult, militarily unrealistic and needlessly provocative for Washington to assert a legitimate expectation of exercising US control in the East and South China seas in the face of Chinese opposition.[1] The primary US objective is not to blunt or contain China's naval expansion, which the United States may not be able or even inclined to do. What concerns Washington is more targeted Chinese claims and efforts to extend sea, air and land control over Taiwan and areas in the East and South China seas that have been nominally independent or uncontrolled. Now that China claims the near seas as internal and sovereign territory, it wants the US military out of those areas – and expects to attain that goal in the not-too-distant future.[2]

Military considerations

The Pentagon has concluded that the US needs, at minimum, a sustainable and selective deterrence-by-denial scheme whereby it can deny China the ability to seize and hold disputed territory.[3] This would call for decisive anti-access and area-denial (A2/AD) capabilities. Denial, of course, does not constitute outright victory, and might not induce China to stop fighting altogether. Accordingly, the Pentagon has conceptualised more aggressive approaches. The two most prominent are the 'Air–Sea Battle' (ASB) concept of neutralising China through pre-emption and strikes on the mainland, and the less escalatory 'offshore control' alternative under which the US and its partners would blockade China's energy and raw-material imports and industrial exports. These options would mainly leverage long-range precision-strike and naval assets respectively, and would not rely operationally on forward bases to any great extent. The force-design plans of the US Marine Corps (USMC) envision Marine Expeditionary Units fighting within the A2/AD bubble.[4] This sounds like a return to 'island-hopping', with such units operating in contested areas from small, distributed bases in the littorals.[5]

A simple denial campaign would seem to have the least prospect for escalation, the highest prospect for success and the lowest degree of reliance on forward bases. It is difficult to determine in the abstract whether the US could hit the Chinese mainland so hard as to neutralise the threat to forward US forces or to induce China to cease fighting. It is also unclear whether a blockade would be effective, and in any case it would seem unachievable without the support of Russia, which would be unlikely to be forthcoming. Both approaches would also risk Chinese nuclear escalation.

Selective and innovative forward deployments, however, certainly could enhance the US ability to deter or compel China. Mobile surface-to-surface precision-strike ballistic missiles – such as the Army Tactical Missile System (in service since 1991) and the Precision Strike Missile slated for deployment in 2023 – operated by US Army or Marine Corps units might, for example, be rotationally placed in the Philippines to hold some of China's artificial islands at risk, as an alternative to more traditional and expensive strike platforms like fighters, long-range bombers and aircraft carriers.[6] This could also help stabilise the US–Philippines strategic relationship. While Filipino President Rodrigo Duterte was notably cool towards close security cooperation with the US, his successor Ferdinand Marcos Jr, taking office in June 2022, is more likely to be open to it. But the leaders of small Indo-Pacific nations are also wary of antagonising Beijing, and most would be reluctant to host long-range American weapons capable of threatening China.[7] In any case, from an operational standpoint such deployments are optional in light of developing capabilities for sea-basing assets such as the High-Mobility Artillery Rocket System (deployed since 2005) and an emerging force design supporting lighter, more mobile and lower-signature USMC postures and deployments that achieve 'the virtues of mass without the vulnerabilities of concentration'.[8]

Whether the US could successfully assert and maintain control over the East and South China seas with or without forward bases is an open question, but the limited nature of US strategic interests versus China's substantially higher stake in establishing regional parity and greater control argue against attempts to do so from a strategic standpoint, irrespective of military feasibility. Accordingly, mutual denial would probably be acceptable. This would not require extraordinary force. Permanent regional basing would be far less important for this purpose than the ability to routinely stage refuelling and resupply operations through regional ports and airfields and to launch fighter strikes from such facilities. This could entail the dispersal of small expeditionary airfields, perhaps clustering groups of several under shared air- and missile-defence umbrellas.[9]

A major regional engagement such as that anticipated in the ASB concept would call for a higher operational tempo than transoceanic long-range missions alone could generate, so land-based regional facilities supporting offensive air operations would still be indispensable. It would be difficult for the US to station combat aircraft on a fixed-contingency basis outside Japan and South Korea; suitable partner fighter/attack bases are few and far between. The most sensible compromise solution appears to be the US Air Force's (USAF) 'Places, not Bases' concept. Under this approach, the air force would expand the network of regional fighter-capable airfields from which it might operate during a crisis using existing expeditionary capabilities, including joint ocean transport and sea-basing, to rapidly convert those airfields into operational fighter or attack bases. The number of feasible 'frontier bases' could increase from 39 to 84 simply by allowing for expeditionary munitions storage using existing capabilities (Military Sealift Command's two squadrons in the Indo-Pacific, at Diego Garcia and the Marianas). The concept has been successfully demonstrated in non-combat contingencies.[10] In an April 2019 exercise, US Indo-Pacific Command's air component dispersed from Andersen Air Force Base in Guam and quickly resumed operations at airfields in Palau, Saipan, Tinian and the Federated States of Micronesia. Under the 2014 Enhanced Defense Cooperation Agreement, the Pentagon is building new facilities at five sites in the Philippines.[11] It has also arranged for access to two air bases in northern Australia, which will expand logistical capabilities and facilitate combined operations with the Australian military. The distances involved in maritime logistical operations in the Indo-Pacific mean that force-protection problems would be less severe than in the Middle East, but could still be significant.[12]

In potentially escalatory scenarios such as a Chinese seizure of sovereign territory, imposition of sea or air control in the East China Sea or South China Sea, or a blockade of Taiwan, there would be no military imperative for US forces to respond rapidly, although it might be desirable or even necessary politically. A Chinese invasion of Taiwan with little warning would undoubtedly require a rapid response, but that could involve stand-off strikes from *Tomahawk* land-attack missiles (TLAMs) or joint air-to-surface stand-off missiles on Chinese forces at a beachhead or in port. Missiles of these kinds could be brought quickly within range by air or naval platforms. Much depends, however, on the quantity of munitions required, since the Mark 41 vertical launch system can only be reloaded in port, limiting the ammunition availability in a crisis. While ships do carry a fair number of canisters, not all will be loaded with TLAMs. Moreover, the feasibility of reversing Chinese attempts at aggrandisement before they are fait accomplis could erode, especially if Beijing increases its regional political traction.

Beijing fields the world's most abundant and capable theatre ballistic-missile arsenal.[13] China has deployed at least two weapons systems, the DF-26 intermediate-range ballistic missile (IRBM) and air-launched land-attack cruise missiles, capable of reaching Guam, which it assesses as central to the regional US force posture.[14] In August 2017, Pyongyang launched an IRBM over the northern Japanese island of Hokkaido. In so doing, it demonstrated an ability to strike not only Japan but also the US base in Guam.[15] In November of the same year, it tested an intercontinental ballistic missile. Guam is nevertheless less vulnerable to US adversaries than South Korea and Japan, and in the near term, these factors favour building up Guam's support and maintenance capabilities, reinforcing its defences and intensifying contingency planning for any kinetic action involving the island.[16] Some 4,100 marines stationed in Okinawa will be redeployed to a new base in Guam starting as early as 2024 and, with 900 additional marines, will make up a 5,000-strong Guam-based contingent. Roughly another 4,800 Okinawa-based marines are slated to be redeployed elsewhere, for a total reduction of marines in Okinawa of about 9,000.[17] These shifts are broadly in line with the longer-term military rationale for pulling US military assets out of the island territory and relying more heavily on US facilities in Australia, Diego Garcia and Singapore and, farther back, Alaska and Hawaii.[18] In April 2020, the USAF withdrew its B-52 strategic bombers from Guam, ending its 16-year Continuous Bomber Presence Mission in favour of the less predictable and more resilient and flexible 'Dynamic Force Employment' concept of operations under which the bombers are based stateside.[19]

There is no realistic prospect that North Korea could conquer and occupy South Korea: while it could devastate its neighbour with artillery, missile and rocket strikes, a ground invasion would be reversed by US and allied forces over time. The key US advantage in any contingency along these lines is its huge arsenal of TLAMs. Because these have proven so useful for decades, the Pentagon has placed a premium on maintaining a qualitative and quantitative advantage that it is unlikely to relinquish.[20] TLAMs constitute the leading edge of the US striking arm for almost any contingency. These missiles are sea-based, inherently mobile and do not require forward bases. Post-Intermediate-Range Nuclear Forces Treaty, the USMC has experimented with firing TLAMs from mobile land-based vertical launch systems for land-attack and anti-ship missions and is reportedly interested in establishing a deployed capability.[21]

Political considerations

Even if, from a military perspective, there are no feasible contingencies that require or justify most of the forces that the US has forward-positioned in East Asia, there are powerful political arguments against reducing some elements of the US basing presence in the Indo-Pacific. The increased flexibility to deploy or redeploy in short order – afforded by the mobility of maritime assets – is not necessarily reassuring to allies. Active and substantial American bases in Japan and South Korea, for example, are essential for reassuring Tokyo and Seoul of the integrity of extended US deterrence vis-à-vis China and North Korea, and for constraining these US allies from pursuing nuclear options of their own. Yet the larger the US force that is staged forward, the more US allies seem to depend on Washington to carry the load. Donald Trump seemed to think that if the US withdrew forces, allies would be compelled to stand up for themselves against US strategic adversaries, and he even suggested at one point that Japan could develop nuclear weapons. Yet his repeated suggestion that the US withdraw troops and assets and leave these allies to rely on the US strategic nuclear deterrent and their own conventional deterrents weakened alliances and has made US re-engagement urgent and a steady US presence more vital.[22] His position made the prospect of US retrenchment, as China continues its rise as a superpower, seem even more likely, and opened the possibility that US allies could react by accommodating Beijing or Pyongyang.[23] In the long term, such political considerations counsel extreme caution about substantially diminishing the forward US presence.

Day-to-day liaison, frequent exercises and the enduring understanding that they can call on each other in relatively short order fosters a familiarity between the US and its allies and partners. But, in the case of Japan, no integrated approach to a potential conflict (that is, no unified command structure, planning or exercising) exists, due substantially to the constraints on military activity built into the Japanese constitution after the Second World War. Japan customarily seems to expect that the US will surge forward and do the bulk of the fighting should an armed conflict begin. Some American analysts have bolstered this assumption by deeming the US bases in Japan indispensable. Ian Easton, for example, makes this claim with respect to the air bases at Kadena, Misawa and Yokota; he further states that the naval bases at Yokosuka and Sasebo and the Marine Corps air stations at Iwakuni and Futenma constitute 'the cornerstone of US power projection in the Indo-Pacific' and are 'irreplaceable' and must be made less vulnerable and more resilient through hardening, dispersal, deception and counter-reconnaissance measures.[24]

Even if Japan cannot be expected to jettison its constitutional military constraints to an extent that would enable it to develop independent deterrent and war-fighting capabilities, making the US presence in Japan leaner would have ancillary political benefits. The stationing of around 50,000 military personnel, Department of Defense civilians and dependents in Okinawa Prefecture has generated decades of environmental, safety, economic and cultural complaints from the locals and provoked anti-base protests in Okinawa and on the mainland. For example, the prospective relocation of Marine Corps Air

Station Futenma to a less congested area within the prefecture, intended to abate concerns about noise and safety risks, has perversely exacerbated community-relations problems due to local politics and years of delays.[25] In autumn 2017, one crash and three emergency landings in Okinawa involving V-22 *Osprey* hybrid aircraft and marine helicopters stoked more agitation for the closing of Futenma.[26] Given the political limitations on combined US–Japanese military operations and the friction produced by Futenma, the argument for closing the base rather than relocating it to an alternate facility under construction on Okinawa – the current plan – may have gradually become stronger. It remains unclear, however, whether entirely removing the USMC aviation capabilities from Japan is militarily viable.

Pyongyang's recent nuclear-weapons and ballistic-missile tests may be an incentive for Tokyo to move more briskly towards a defensive military capability less dependent on the US.[27] China's growing assertiveness and the erratic US foreign policy under Trump has also prompted Japan to pay more attention to deterrence.[28] As prime minister, Abe Shinzo (2012–20) showed a greater appetite than his predecessors for stretching the legal definition of self-defence forces, which Japan's 'peace constitution' permits.[29] If the US had fewer forward forces, Tokyo might be more inclined to take on greater military responsibility in the region.[30] Keeping a small 'tripwire' force stationed forward in Japan would show that the US had a material stake in its security while also impelling the Japanese to accept the burden of fighting early and hard – or, alternatively, to avoid conflict situations altogether through appeasement.

The US force in South Korea, comprising about 31,000 personnel (down from over 40,000 during the Cold War), is essentially a tripwire deterrent of this kind. An even smaller force, backed by South Korean-manned short-range weaponry for reducing North Korean artillery, the Terminal High Altitude Area Defense missile-defence system, and a constant US naval presence in the Korean Peninsula, might function as an effective deterrent while inducing greater military participation in regional defence by Japan and more constructive diplomatic intervention with Pyongyang on China's part.[31]

Although the principal political utility of permanent bases is as a public demonstration of alliance strength and commitment, they also facilitate combined military exercises, which could discourage Chinese regional assertiveness. But the US would need to undertake far more extensive combined planning and exercises than it has customarily done (even before Trump suspended such activities in 2018–19 to placate Kim Jong-un), and press allies to reduce their own inherent vulnerabilities, to generate a credible combined war-fighting capability and deterrent. Even if Japan follows through with a somewhat more extroverted defence posture, such a capability probably would not be achievable in Japan due to residual constitutional constraints. While it is plausible with respect to South Korea, it may be less desirable given North Korean hypersensitivity to US–South Korean combined exercises as well as the American forward presence, and the desire to dissuade Pyongyang from continuing its nuclear and missile programmes. One way forward could be the 'double freeze' approach proposed by China whereby North Korea would suspend its programmes in exchange for US suspension of combined exercises and a diminished US presence in South Korea.[32] In theory, this course could incentivise South Korea to eventually increase its self-reliance. But, at least in the short term, it would be more likely to reduce South Korea's readiness and willingness to fight. In any case, in the wake of Trump's failed attempts to gain concessions from North Korea on its nuclear-weapons programme by unilaterally suspending exercises in 2018 and 2019, this now seems politically infeasible. Facilitation of combined exercises remains a strong argument for retention of permanent bases.

While it seems unlikely that either Japan or South Korea would field nuclear weapons even if their confidence in the US were to wane, the Trump administration's insular sensibilities and North Korea's march towards an intercontinental nuclear capability and regional brinkmanship have made such a scenario marginally more plausible.[33] Despite the conventional wisdom that nuclear proliferation is bad, some have suggested that there could be a strategic upside to a nuclear-armed Seoul and Tokyo.[34] If uncertainty about the US commitment to its allies were to increase, China and North Korea might well find Japanese and South Korean second-strike nuclear capabilities to be as much or more credible a deterrent than American nuclear weapons. If Japan and South Korea had survivable nuclear retaliatory forces and the US did not have major bases forward, there could be even greater strategic stability.[35] Fortunately, in any case, it now appears less plausible that the US will abandon extended deterrence.

Given the global economic centrality of the Indo-Pacific and China's standing intention to challenge US regional military primacy, it is unlikely that any American administration would be inclined to substantially downgrade the United States' military presence or activities in the region. The US policy of maintaining a geopolitically balanced Indo-Pacific against China's apparent quest for regional hegemony is unlikely to change, requires an active and substantial US naval and air presence, and needs to accommodate the possibility of major armed conflict with China. Yet new vulnerabilities, especially Guam's, counsel greater dispersal and perhaps some curtailment of permanent US military assets within the region.[36] The US has achieved its Obama-era target of allocating 60% of its naval assets to the Asia-Pacific by 2020.[37] Other things being equal, this might be enough to mitigate any alarm on the part of US allies and partners over marginal reductions in the US permanent forward presence, affording the US some latitude for doing so in the Indo-Pacific. And despite the reallocation of US naval assets to the region and superior American technology and training, China has far more vessels in the Indo-Pacific than the US does.[38] These countervailing factors cut against a major reduction of the United States' military activity in the region in the short and medium term.

CHAPTER FIVE

Optimising US regional footprints: Europe

The post-9/11 age of terror has now given way to a new era of great-power competition. If US forward-deployed forces in the Middle East, where such competition is largely indirect, should be maintained at roughly current levels (see Chapter Three), there is a strong case, even before taking into account the 2022 Ukrainian–Russian war, that heavier deployments, especially army ground units, should be maintained or enhanced in Europe, where confrontations between NATO and Russia could be particularly consequential to regional stability and the Atlantic alliance.[1] The US forward presence in Europe steadily decreased after its premise – defending NATO allies from a conventional attack by Soviet and Warsaw Pact forces and, more tacitly, reassuring Europeans that the German state would not cause trouble again – effectively disappeared with the end of the Cold War. New security challenges such as neighbourhood ethnic conflict, terrorism and proliferation materialised, to be sure, and the residual, but still formidable and clearly energised, Russian military threat limited the degree to which US forces could be withdrawn. Even so, the American redeployment was substantial, and accelerated in

2004, with the completion of the classified Integrated Global Posture and Basing Strategy and the publication of the George W. Bush administration's Global Posture Review.[2]

Before the end of Bush's second term, the 1st Infantry Division had relocated to the United States and plans were in place for a similar redeployment of the 1st Armored Division. The Obama administration eventually decided to continue with the broad outlines of the Bush plan, leaving only the 2nd Cavalry Regiment and the 173rd Airborne Brigade as forward-stationed ground manoeuvre units in Europe.[3] Between 2014 and 2020, however, the US forward presence actually increased as rotational forward-deployed heavy armour and aviation capabilities were returned to US European Command.

Russian revanchism

Although the Russian military is only a small fraction of its peak Cold War size, Russia's aggression in Ukraine, including the annexation of Crimea in 2014 and unprovoked war in 2022, has not just put a hard brake on further US military withdrawal from Europe but prompted its open-ended reversal. Moscow has, moreover, increased defence budgets and intensified military-modernisation plans. This has instilled a sense of urgency within NATO about enhancing the US military presence in Europe and fortifying the Alliance's deterrent and war-fighting capabilities.[4] The overwhelming consensus is that the overall correlation of forces still strongly favours NATO, and that its size, firepower, air supremacy and superior technology would enable it prevail in a major war with Russia.[5] But doubts have arisen about NATO's ability to defend the Baltic states in the event of a Russian attack, which the invasion of Ukraine has (despite revealing shortcomings in Russian capabilities) made appear more likely.[6] Essentially, the speed with which Russia could act would allow it to achieve a fait accompli before sufficient NATO forces could respond.[7] These doubts were reinforced by the 2019 IISS scenario-based 'Defending Europe' study of European capability requirements, which concluded that European NATO allies would be hard pressed, with conventional forces and without US help, to repel and reverse a Russian conquest of Lithuania and part of Poland.[8] That scenario posited a previous US withdrawal from NATO. But even with a continued US commitment, this risk would remain salient in the absence of robust in-theatre US capabilities and infrastructure.[9] In 2021–22, Russia's recognition of the Donetsk and Luhansk regions as independent republics subject to Russian military intervention, and subsequent invasion of Ukraine, emphatically validated worries about a potential Russian attempt to usurp Ukraine and roll back NATO.

IISS defence analysts have concluded that, while decreasing the permanent US overseas presence might afford Washington greater flexibility in responding to threats and contingencies and pose lower risks of escalation, permanent forward-deployed forces ensure the strongest Alliance cohesion and deterrent effect.[10] At the operational level, RAND researchers have determined that surged crisis deployments to contested areas are less successful than substantial permanent deployments near but outside the borders of the states targeted in securing desired political results for those states – for example, in reversing putative faits accomplis.[11]

The eight NATO Force Integration Units in Bulgaria, Estonia, Hungary, Latvia, Lithuania, Poland, Romania and Slovakia and the four battalion-strength components of the Enhanced Forward Presence (EFP) provisionally function as effective tripwire deterrents. But consolidating deterrence would require in-theatre forces quickly deployable once the wire is tripped to stave off advancing Russian forces. Otherwise, using Kaliningrad as an anti-access and area-denial (A2/AD) outpost,

Russia might be tempted to try to overwhelm a Baltic nation and deliver the fait accompli.

With Crimea under its control, since 2014 Russia has been seeking to render its severely degraded Black Sea Fleet capable of executing A2/AD operations to project naval power into the Mediterranean.[12] The centrepiece of the Russian approach is the so-called bastion strategy. Towards the end of the Cold War, the Soviet Union employed surface combat vessels and aircraft operating from hardened bases to protect its submarine-launched nuclear deterrent in the Barents Sea and Sea of Okhotsk rather than have its navy confront the West on open water. Following this model, Crimea could serve as a naval bastion to provide protection for a modernised Black Sea Fleet and the development of a Mediterranean squadron.[13] Russia aimed to spend US$2.3 billion on infrastructure and 80 new ships for its Black Sea Fleet by 2020. While it did not meet its ambitious ship target, it did make significant progress in upgrading the fleet and fortifying Crimea's anti-access capabilities. Crimea's location, and the long range of some of Russia's anti-access weapons and delivery platforms, make the peninsula an effective base for offensive operations.[14]

Russia's anti-access capabilities in the Black Sea include simple contact sea mines at the low end and sophisticated supersonic land-based, air-launched, submarine-based and ship-based anti-ship cruise missiles at the high end. Furthermore, Russia can bar access to the Black Sea not only to NATO and American ships, but also to their aircraft. Russia's S-400 missile-defence system using 40N6 missiles – as of early 2021, accepted for service, though perhaps not yet deployed – could bring down manned aircraft, precision-guided munitions and cruise missiles up to 400 kilometres away. One of Russia's first military moves in Crimea after the takeover, specifically in response to US ships entering the Black Sea, was to deploy *Bastion*-P anti-ship missile systems equipped with the P-800 *Oniks* missile and S-300P anti-aircraft missile systems. The move was a clear signal to NATO that Russia would resist any Western military effort to contest the annexation of Crimea, though there was little chance of this. Soon after the takeover, Moscow announced plans to base Tupolev Tu-142 and Ilyushin Il-38 maritime-patrol and anti-submarine aircraft there, though it remained unclear as of early 2022 whether that had happened.

In the near future, Russia will probably introduce new platforms that further enhance its A2/AD capabilities and further secure Crimea as a bastion. The most formidable of these is likely to be six planned *Varshavyanka*-class submarines – improved versions of the *Kilo*-class submarine, which was itself one of the best diesel-electric submarines ever built. Submarines are uniquely stealthy and flexible, capable of gathering intelligence and of engaging in anti-surface warfare, anti-submarine warfare and land attacks. The new submarines, deployed to the Black Sea, will be able to threaten bases and command centres as well as shipping in the region.[15]

A more dangerous development is the potential basing of strategic bombers in Crimea. In March 2015, Russian officials announced that ten Tu-22M3 *Backfire* bombers would be deployed to Crimea during 'snap drills' in response to large-scale NATO exercises in Central and Eastern Europe.[16] These should be valuable assets for Russia in the Black Sea. During the Cold War, the Soviets deployed the *Backfire*, a long-range strategic bomber, to target US carrier strike groups and NATO maritime forces. Though an old weapons platform, unlike other Soviet-era systems it has been updated and now anchors Russian air-force maritime strike units.

As an anti-access platform, the *Backfire* could represent a potent threat to NATO and US ships, bases and command centres in the Black Sea and Eastern Mediterranean. Moscow is liable to utilise them to try to intimidate and blackmail weaker NATO members. Certainly, their contemplated deployment and clear status as anti-access assets signals to the West that Russia intends to stay in Crimea and can effectively confront NATO and US vessels and project long-range air power in the Black Sea.[17]

One of Russia's most potent battlefield weapons is the *Iskander*-M tactical short-range ballistic missile, with a declared range of 500 km. This is a sophisticated weapons system developed after the end of the Cold War to comply with the Intermediate-Range Nuclear Forces (INF) Treaty and to improve on outdated tactical missiles like the *Scud*. The *Iskander* was conceived as a battlefield support weapon for targeting relatively close adversary platforms, including command centres, long-range artillery and military bases. Russia's nuclear policy contemplates the use of tactical nuclear weapons to compensate for weaknesses in conventional military capabilities under a concept sometimes known as 'escalate to de-escalate'.[18] When Putin implicitly threatened nuclear retaliation against outside parties directly interfering in the Ukrainian–Russian war, it was that aspect of the policy he was alluding to.[19] *Iskander* missiles can deliver small tactical nuclear weapons with a high degree of accuracy, and could therefore cover a land grab by Russia against NATO member states. In 2014, the US publicly accused Russia of breaching the INF Treaty by developing a new cruise-missile version of this weapon with a range greater than 500 km, and the US formally withdrew from the treaty in August 2019.

Russia has warned that it would deploy *Iskander* missiles to counter US missile-defence systems deployed in Poland and Romania. A missile brigade based in Kaliningrad has been re-equipped with *Iskander*-M ballistic missiles but not, as of early 2022 (as far as open sources have revealed), longer-range cruise missiles like the 9M729. From Kaliningrad, *Iskander*-M missiles could threaten or attack pre-positioned NATO trip-wire forces in the Baltic states, Poland and Romania and forces sent to reinforce them. From Crimea, these missiles could reach all those targets except Baltic-based EFP units. Thus, the development of Crimea as a naval bastion in the Black Sea may dilute the effectiveness of the measures NATO has undertaken so far, including the EFP, Very High Readiness Joint Task Force (VJTF) and enhanced NATO Response Force (eNRF), to reassure eastern allies and bolster the NATO deterrent. The A2/AD capabilities that Russia has deployed or could deploy in Kaliningrad have the potential to stymie NATO expeditionary forces in the Baltic states by increasing the potential cost of entry to sea lanes and economic resources and applying coercive pressure, allowing Russia to dominate the early stages of a prospective conflict.[20] In light of these developing Russian capabilities, the conventional land and sea deterrence posture of the Alliance on the eastern flank may require rethinking.

There is a conventional-force imbalance in Russia's favour on NATO's eastern flank.[21] While NATO militaries have focused on fielding lighter forces that can be easily deployed out of area in stability operations, Russia has been concentrating on generating a combined-arms force stressing mobility and firepower in larger-scale operations, improving the quality of its forces through targeted recruitment and modernisation, and internalising lessons from deployments in Ukraine and Syria. In addition, the highest density of Russia's most capable ground and air forces is in its Western Military District, bordering NATO allies Estonia, Latvia and Lithuania, which have very small national conventional forces. Finally, Russia's internal rail and road networks in principle afford it a significant time–distance advantage in massing forces during the opening stages of a crisis, though using them too takes time. The upshot is that Russia's military-logistical capabilities and thick A2/AD capabilities afford it a significant advantage in conflicts between mechanised forces close to its borders. Russia, however, may have exaggerated its A2/AD capabilities, mainly the S-400 air-defence system, the *Bastion*-P anti-ship system and the *Iskander* ballistic missile.[22] Furthermore, its ground forces' conspicuously poor performance in the 2022 Ukrainian–Russian war suggests that Western observers have overestimated the operational effectiveness of its military-modernisation programme.[23]

A robust presence

NATO has the resources, personnel and equipment for an effective conventional deterrent vis-à-vis Russia on NATO's eastern border, but this requires a robust American presence in Europe, including in the east, where it has never existed.[24] This is implicitly acknowledged in the US Army Europe initiative known as *Atlantic Resolve*, in place since April 2014, whereby the army has rotated armoured, aviation and logistics task forces from stateside bases to forward locations in Europe for nine months at a time to demonstrate its commitment to NATO.[25] Overseen by a rotating divisional forward headquarters in Poznan, Poland, the programme has focused on increasing readiness in the east in light of Russia's posture.[26] Yet relatively long-term rotational deployments alone might not be enough to firmly deter Russia in the Baltic states.[27] In the broader context of resupply and reassurance, as well as capability development in Europe, the IISS's 'Defending Europe' exercise reinforced this point.

Since mid-2017, NATO contingency planning for the east has centred on the 40,000-strong eNRF – including a command-and-control element based on a deployable joint task-force headquarters, the 'spearhead' VJTF, the Initial Follow-on Forces Group whose deployment would follow the VJTF's, and the Response Forces Pool for reinforcements. The permanently assigned elements are based in Western Europe, and its lead headquarters is Allied Joint Force Command Brunssum in the Netherlands. As of 2020, most of its elements were not American.[28] One option for enhancing the current posture may be to substantially bolster forward deployments, with tanks and other armoured assets regaining prominence. This would call for robust basing infrastructure relatively close to the most likely flashpoints in Eastern Europe to ensure a timely response to a Russian provocation. The US has no permanent bases in Eastern Europe, but it has enhanced its rotational presence in Poland and elsewhere.[29] A permanent American base in Eastern Europe might, however, antagonise Russia. Moreover, NATO would have to preclude Russian long-range pre-emptive strikes – in particular, with *Iskander* missiles – on forward-deployed troops and assets, perhaps through US missile-defence systems.

Whatever the precise geographical details, NATO needs sufficient forces based forward to deter Russia from attempting to achieve a fait accompli in the Baltic states. It would make sense for NATO to continue to enhance its rotational presence in Poland and the Baltic states to extend the reaction time available for reinforcement in a contingency. This could be part of a larger defensive, denial-based strategy for preserving the status quo, augmented by deployed precision-strike assets holding Kaliningrad at risk, to establish a NATO A2/AD bubble over the eastern region. Such assets could include post-INF Treaty ground-based intermediate-range missiles, but there are also less provocative and escalatory options.[30] While a stronger posture could involve a heavily enhanced US rotational presence and dynamic force employment in or near the Baltic states, it would be prudent for NATO to keep forward-deployed NATO tripwire forces lean, rely on national governments to build up their military capabilities and exploit the Alliance's strategic depth by situating main US forces in the rear while improving transportation and logistics infrastructure and capabilities for getting them to the action. Some Eastern European allies might not see basing US forces out of harm's way, as it were, as maximising reassurance that the US will be there for them. Such an approach, however, would limit vulnerability, increase operational flexibility and decrease the time it takes to flow forces to contested areas.[31] It would require that the US maintain its current basing infrastructure and deployments in Europe.

CHAPTER SIX

Conclusion

Fatigue with America's 'endless wars' has inclined the US public and policy community to favour reducing global military activities and overseas presence.[1] Donald Trump was elected on a platform to do just that. But Trump's reckless foreign policy diminished confidence in America, and with it international security, to such a degree that it now has less freedom of action to address that impulse. The Biden administration's priority is to resurrect and bolster the United States' reputation among its allies and adversaries for the sake of international security rather than to moderate US commitments. Overseas bases are a key element of the reassurance required.

Meanwhile, US strategic imperatives and geopolitical realities impose restraints in every theatre. The strategic fluidity prevailing in the Middle East – in particular, Iran's regional activities, uncertainty about reviving the Joint Comprehensive Plan of Action (JCPOA) and the potential for jihadist resurgence – counsels maintaining forward-deployed forces in the Middle East at roughly the current level. Similarly, while current forward-deployed forces in the Indo-Pacific need not necessarily be increased, neither should they be reduced. In light of Russia's confrontational posture towards NATO (rendered credible by its annexation of Crimea and strategically seismic war in Ukraine), as well as NATO's short- and medium-term inability to repel and possibly deter further Russian aggrandisement without quickly employable US capabilities along with European NATO members' rising uncertainty about the US commitment during the Trump years, the American presence in Europe should be increased and expanded eastward.

The Indo-Pacific

Trump's implicit plans for military pullback from the Indo-Pacific appear to have been substantially stymied by the rising nuclear and ballistic-missile threats from North Korea, China's apparent determination to consolidate claims over the Senkaku/Diaoyu islands and its other claims over maritime territory in the South China Sea, as well as its continued pursuit of Taiwan's forced reunification. More broadly, China's military strength and regional ambitions are likely to increase over the next 25 years, reinforcing general constraints on US withdrawal. Washington will likely remain inclined to pressure Beijing itself to hold North Korea in check in conjunction with the standing US strategic deterrent and intermittent shows of force (such as surging carrier strike groups to the region and sending long-range bombers near North Korean waters) at crisis points. This posture amounts to a crude form of offshore balancing and does not seem sustainable. While Washington should encourage US allies and partners – Japan in particular – to develop more robust capabilities that enable them to sustain a greater share of the defence burden, affirming an enduring US commitment to the region will allow them to do so with confidence and deliberation. This will require a continued US forward presence, but increased vulnerabilities counsel modifications.

The US deployment in South Korea, to some extent vulnerable by design, has functioned as a tripwire deterrent, staving off a major North Korean conventional attack. Some observers have suggested that North Korea wants nuclear weapons in order to discourage the US from intervening in a future invasion of South Korea, thus neutralising the tripwire deterrent.[2] In the meantime, though, since the status quo provides substantial strategic stability, the US deployment in South Korea ought to stay in place. If local US forces were deployed only in Japan, and not in South Korea, it would be more feasible for North Korean forces to invade the South without triggering a US response. Broader deterrence against China as well as North Korea may not require so many US forces in Japan, especially if Japan continues to relax constitutional restrictions on the use of military forces and expands its capabilities, which appears likely even after the departure of Abe Shinzo in 2020.[3]

Farther south, US forward-deployed forces are not ideally configured to deal with Chinese encroachment and require greater dispersal. Washington's Enhanced Defense Cooperation Agreement and joint base construction with the Philippines and new forward operating locations in Australia help in this regard, but budgetary and political factors as well as command-and-control issues limit their utility. Multilateral military efforts like the US–Japan–Australia exercises to ensure freedom of navigation and protect overflight rights will remain useful for enhancing defence cooperation and inter-operability at the operational level. Strategically, though, the US and its allies and partners need to be ready for potential conflict with China and, therefore, to stage anti-access and area-denial (A2/AD) (including maritime denial) operations closer to China's coast and, *in extremis*, onshore air–sea operations.[4]

At the operational level, the pressing question is how best to configure US forces in the region to shape the battlespace and prepare for possible conflict while not alarming adversaries – in particular, North Korea and China – and hence hastening actual armed conflict. Many US strategic objectives in the Indo-Pacific are achievable via long-range precision strike (LRPS), which allows for a degree of pullback that would decrease vulnerability. The key inhibitor of redeployment rearward is the difficulty of reassuring allies and partners that Washington's regional commitment to their defence and protection will remain intact. As the saying goes, trust cannot be surged. But there may be other means besides forward physical bases to establish trust. It could perhaps be advanced by emphasising LRPS as an increasingly important element of US doctrine and planning on a declaratory basis, and demonstrating its operational credibility.

In 2014, two B-1B *Lancer* bombers flew a non-stop roundtrip from Ellsworth Air Force Base in California to strike targets near Guam, covering over 20,000 kilometres in 30 hours.[5] Yet the 17 hours from base to target, fast for intercontinental manned aircraft, is significantly longer than a response from locally based air assets would take. Hypersonic conventional weapons would close the gap, but they could also reduce strategic and crisis stability, so substituting them for regionally deployed assets may not be an ideal option – especially in the absence of a viable arms-control framework.[6] While America's first resort in a conflict in the Indo-Pacific would be to air and naval power, the potential need for ground forces – recognised in the US Marine Corps' new look at the prospect of island hopping – is not negligible. Thus, reassurance in the form of a military presence at land bases in the region remains important.

The Pentagon tends to favour forward-stationed rather than rotational forces in the region due to the long-standing base-centred alliances with Japan and South Korea. Senior officers nevertheless emphasise the need to disperse assets and apply a more expeditionary concept to the US regional presence in order to enhance flexibility and decrease vulnerability. This 'light and lean' approach involves relatively small units deploying in dispersed locations, which takes advantage of communications and logistical functions such as replenishing fuel and munitions. The approach does court some potential drawbacks. Mobility in a contested environment should not be taken as a given, nor should access to the electromagnetic spectrum at the level US forces might need. In any case, China is likely to exert diplomatic and economic pressure on potential US hosts to discourage their cooperation. Nevertheless, there is scope for some degree of American success in effectuating this reorientation. The bases involved need not be permanent, the premium being on overall troop mobilisation and strategic capacity.[7] The cross-serving and logistics arrangements used in peacetime to build cooperation and inter-operability could also enable the inflow of US equipment in a crisis (rather than a permanent deployment), alongside infrastructure enhancements that the US has advocated such as runways and aprons.

Rising concerns about the vulnerability of US bases in Japan and China's rising A2/AD capabilities could lend momentum to this shift in approach.[8] The US might see fit, among other measures, to further strengthen, diplomatically and operationally, its alliance with Australia.[9] In April 2019, the US deployed 1,700 marines to Darwin for training and exercises, and in July 2019 the total reached the target of 2,500 set by the Obama administration.[10] At least on a political level, the AUKUS arrangement intended to facilitate Australia's procurement and deployment of nuclear submarines signals a tighter US–Australia alliance.

The Middle East

The active US naval presence in the Indo-Pacific required by the US policy of maintaining geopolitical balance, in opposition to China's quest for regional hegemony, need not disrupt US basing calculations for the Middle East. The question of how far forward forces should be positioned in the region once the major contingencies in Iraq and Afghanistan ended has been looming for 20 years. Now that those situations have essentially wound down, the question has become more urgent. Several factors support a basing dispensation close to the status quo, including the strategic importance of regional stability for the sake of a stable global oil market; the likelihood that smaller counter-terrorism contingencies, such as a resurgence of Islamic State (ISIS) or al-Qaeda, and the need to protect oil tankers from Iranian attacks in the Gulf will arise from time to time; and the possibility of a major military confrontation with Iran.[11]

But many personnel and assets deployed in Bahrain and Qatar were there to support operations in Iraq and Afghanistan; the steady-state presence in the absence of such contingencies will be much smaller, allowing either a consolidation of the US regional base presence or sustaining access with residual capability at each existing base. Given the heavy requirements for resources in the Indo-Pacific, the Pentagon's Central Command's (CENTCOM) contingency-based orientation and resulting preference for rotational personnel are likely to continue.[12] A trend towards employing special-forces units rather than Brigade Combat Teams (BCT) (the standard unit) may bolster movement away from forward-deployed forces in favour of a more surge-oriented posture.

The US appears destined to remain a status quo power in the Middle East by default, at least in the medium term. In fact, Washington may even be prone to flirt with revisionism in the region by stoking strategic competition between the Gulf Sunni Arab states and Iran, and to continue to try to roll back Iran to some degree. Syria and Iraq remain likely focal points, given the possibility of a resurgence of ISIS as a consequence of the abrupt US withdrawal. A less likely but still plausible focus of rollback efforts would be Yemen; the Trump administration's disavowal of the JCPOA allowed the Islamic Revolutionary Guard Corps (IRGC) to regain any strategic traction that it might have lost and to continue its aggression in these locales.

These factors favour maintaining the status quo regarding bases. The US could, to be sure, stage and execute periodic limited military operations from mobile naval platforms, as it did with the *Tomahawk* land-attack missile strikes on Syria in April 2017. Even a sustained air campaign could be waged in this way if the US were hard-pressed. But US-led anti-ISIS air operations also made heavy use of land bases in Jordan, Kuwait and the United Arab Emirates (UAE). Furthermore, carrier-based air campaigns are difficult to sustain across maintenance cycles. Moreover, Washington's regional allies and partners perceive a need for sustained American military capabilities and action in the region due to recent failures of US deterrence with respect to Iran and ISIS, and active, low-intensity threats in the form of Iranian proxies (such as IRGC-backed Shia militias and Hizbullah) and Sunni jihadists. Accordingly, and in light of the rebalance to Asia, allies and partners in the Middle East may be less amenable than those in the Indo-Pacific to the soaring promise of stand-off LRPS as a substitute for a more reassuring forward US regional basing presence that deters more reliably.[13]

Particularly in light of the US withdrawal of *Patriot* missile-defence batteries from Iraq, Jordan, Kuwait and Saudi Arabia in 2021, regional partners will need to be reassured of a durable US presence for deterring Iranian actions and capable of responding readily to Iranian and jihadist aggression. Even advocates of strategic restraint agree that the US ought to retain one major air and naval hub in the region.[14] It would be preferable for the US to maintain its Combined Air Operations Center and air assets at Al Udeid Air Base in Qatar and Naval Support Activity Bahrain, with Al Dhafra Air Base in the UAE and Kuwait or Duqm in Oman as respective fallbacks, depending on political circumstances. In any case, the US permanent-basing presence would remain largely the same in scope, even if rearranged.

Nevertheless, successful demonstrations that long-range precision capabilities might effectively redress tangible and proximate threats could reduce regional players' demand for a large American presence. Extensive drone operations in Afghanistan and Pakistan, and more limited ones in Libya, Somalia and Yemen, have shown that precision strikes can contain terrorism, or 'mow the grass', by disrupting command structures. While the promise of LRPS would not extend to counter-insurgency, there is not likely to be much taste for such operations in the wake of the fraught experiences of Iraq and Afghanistan.[15] That said, it seems doubtful that LRPS could easily counter Iranian mine warfare and littoral operations and, therefore, unlikely that it could credibly enable the US to secure the Strait of Hormuz against Iranian provocations without fighting inside the strait itself.

Europe

Ongoing uncertainty about Moscow's intentions on NATO's eastern flank – intensified by its military exercises in Belarus, stealthy insinuation into Slavic and Orthodox Christian parts of the Balkans and invasion and occupation of parts of Ukraine – call for further development of US A2/AD, quick-reaction and reinforcement capabilities.[16] These, in turn, require a steady and in some respects enhanced US presence in the region. The 4,500 soldiers in four multinational battlegroups of the Enhanced Forward Presence are essentially a tripwire force, and its strength as a forward deterrent depends on how quickly NATO, and in particular its Very High Readiness Joint Task Force (VJTF), could reinforce them from rear areas – a point heavily stressed in NATO's biannual *Saber Guardian* exercises in Bulgaria, Hungary and Romania.[17]

In 2016, former NATO secretary general Anders Fogh Rasmussen said that the VJTF was insufficient to deter Russia from undertaking selective aggression against Eastern and Central European NATO member states, and that a reinforced Allied physical presence was required. Even if the VJTF could mobilise and commence flowing reinforcements to the eastern flank within 48 hours of warning, and the enhanced NATO Response Force (eNRF) – at a strength of 40,000 troops – could deploy soon thereafter, eastern members' protection against Russian military occupation could not be assured. The VJTF and eNRF are rotational entities and have no permanent bases or headquarters. Rasmussen advocated locating permanent NATO bases near its eastern perimeter.[18] The most logical place, with regard to the trade-off between vulnerability and responsiveness, is Germany, which has long hosted more US military facilities than any other European country and offers the advantages of pre-existing infrastructure, military-to-military relationships and political familiarity. The Biden administration's freeze on withdrawing 12,000 US troops from Germany, originally ordered by Trump, implicitly recognised this.[19] Since 2016, NATO has also established two new operational-logistics commands: Joint Forces Command in Norfolk, Virginia, responsible for securing transatlantic sea lines of communication, and the Joint Support and Enabling Command in Ulm, Germany, responsible for securing the rear area of operations and implementing forward deployments to the joint-operations area. The latter location is consistent with an emerging pattern of treating Poland as a staging ground with Germany centrally located in the rear.[20]

Heightened NATO threat perceptions vis-à-vis Russia, and Germany's more forward-leaning defence policy due to the Ukrainian–Russian war (including an instantaneous increase to the NATO defence-spending target of 2% of GDP, unseen in Germany in the twenty-first century), have only reinforced this dispensation. About a month into the war, NATO Secretary General Jens Stoltenberg also announced that four new battle-groups would be deployed to Bulgaria, Hungary, Romania and Slovakia alongside the four existing ones in Poland and the Baltic states, that they too would remain there as long as necessary, and that NATO would have to 'reset … deterrence and defence for the longer term'.[21] Between January and March 2022, the US increased the number of American troops on the continent from 80,000 to 100,000, and increased deployments to Germany, Poland and Romania.[22] While any substantial US basing presence on NATO's eastern flank would be unduly provocative and destabilising, the compulsion to periodically deploy more NATO troops forward is likely to bolster the need for a heightened US presence in Europe, probably centred in Germany.

The VJTF's mobilisation time is longer than Russia's, due to Russia's relative proximity to the notional battlespace and NATO's cumbersome decision-making apparatus. The VJTF can, moreover, only be dispatched to one contingency at a time, and could be unavailable in a crisis.[23] Seven European allies have agreed to supply most of the VJTF's land-force manpower, while the US has pledged to provide key enablers, such as air power for intelligence, surveillance and reconnaissance and airlift as well as long-range-strike and naval capabilities.[24] While NATO hopes to provide air power on an integrated basis, it is, in the words of one analyst, 'addicted to US support' and is likely to rely inordinately on US assets even after the introduction of the American F-35 Joint Strike Fighter into some European air forces.[25]

A European Activity Set (EAS) was originally established for use in the Baltic states, Bulgaria, Poland and Romania by the rotational US European Command (EUCOM) armoured BCT.[26] From 2017, however, EUCOM armoured BCT rotations instead used their own equipment, deployed from the continental US, and the EAS was absorbed into army pre-positioned stocks. The overall holding of armoured vehicles (including *Abrams* tanks, *Bradley* fighting vehicles, mobile howitzers and other artillery) is currently sized to equip nearly two armoured BCTs, and European Deterrence Initiative budget documentation funds a build-up to two armoured BCT sets and two artillery-brigade sets. But beyond the assessment that US capabilities are critical to European defence, Russia is historically accustomed to dealing with an Alliance that is politically and operationally anchored by the US, and it is far less likely to be deterred by one that is not.[27] The symbol of that anchor is the permanent US physical presence in Europe, and, especially in light of the Ukrainian–Russian war, it is likely to need to be not just sustained but enhanced.

Prospects

Political scientist Christopher Fettweis has noted that the Roman emperor Hadrian, most famous for the seemingly exclusionary frontier wall he built in northern Britain, was a foreign-policy realist who made the Roman Empire's retrenchment a strategic asset despite 'substantial psychological barriers'.[28] His popular predecessor, Trajan, had presided over exceptional and aggressive expansion. However, Hadrian saw imperial aggression as a source of vulnerability, and under him 'the military instrument of Roman power took a back seat to diplomacy and economics'.[29] He stopped the legions from expanding into new territories and withdrew from Trajan's conquests east of the Euphrates in modern Iraq, but keeping his troops garrisoned inside the empire's frontiers did not preclude sending them forward to fight the presumed barbarians if necessary. Thus, Roman armies improved their readiness and strengthened Rome's deterrent. While the intent of Hadrian's many walls – he also fortified the Rhine and Danube frontiers – is disputed, Fettweis suggests that they were 'manifestations of restraint', making it 'clear on both sides that expansion would not be taking place on Hadrian's watch' and 'sending messages to the peoples beyond that they had little to fear from the superpower on the other side'.[30] As such, they reflected a doctrinal stand against imperial overextension, and against what would now be called 'Lippmann gaps' – that is, shortfalls in the power and resources needed to meet established commitments.[31]

The US now faces such shortfalls. As most US military planners would candidly admit, the US military, despite being by far the most powerful in the world, would be hard-pressed if called on to thwart, simultaneously or in rapid sequence, a Chinese assertion of naval primacy in the South China Sea or an invasion of Taiwan, Russian Finlandisation of a Baltic country, or an attempt by Iran to become nuclear-weapons capable. Yet addressing Lippmann gaps through contraction would require a fundamental re-examination of foreign commitments, including alliances and foreign assistance, not just forward deployments. This might be advisable in principle.[32] But it does not yet appear achievable in practice.[33] And retrenchment would not be a solution everywhere. While the US may be saddled with burdensome commitments and unreliable partners without a clear strategy in the Middle East, the strategic advantages of robust US engagement in Asia and Europe are clear. There also remain fine and particular operational balances to be struck in each of the three main areas of operation.

In the Middle East, the US will be facing different threats than it will in East Asia, where its burgeoning LRPS capability would be more relevant. In Europe, in-theatre personnel strength and ground-deployment speed will be uniquely critical issues.

Trump's muddled foreign policy, moreover, complicated any attempt at selective retrenchment. Recognising a strategic Lippmann gap, the Obama administration attempted a gradual and orderly reorientation through the strategic rebalance to Asia, a measured pullback from the Middle East and the even-handed 'reset' of the US–Russia relationship. While the reset had stalled by 2017, the other elements remained viable. Had Trump continued in that vein, and adopted a similarly considered grand strategy of restraint, the US might have been able to advance an offshore-balancing approach that would involve less robust forward deployments while still maintaining Allied confidence. But Trump's attempts at strategic contraction were distinctly shambolic and strategically incoherent. His crypto-isolationist musings, denigration of traditional US alliances and acquiescence to Russian revanchism prompted signals from regional partners that the US should revert to the status quo. The failure of Trump's initiatives to dispose decisively of immediate strategic challenges may make it harder, rather than easier, for Washington to relax legacy commitments in practice, beneficial though that might be in theory. At this stage, pulling back forces wholesale might leave America facing a regional conflict that it could have deterred, and for which it has become less prepared.[34]

The Pentagon's most recent Global Posture Review, completed in November 2021, stressed that the US was compelled to return to the normal American practice of determining its military posture around the world according to America's strategic alignment. This meant prioritising the Indo-Pacific while strengthening NATO's deterrent vis-à-vis

Russia and maintaining a residual presence in the Middle East sufficient to preserve regional stability, respond to crises and reassure allies and partners.[35] Understandably, that outcome seemed to some to be dispiritingly staid and generic, reflecting little more than a return to the status quo ante Trump and shirking issues such as small-and-dispersed versus large-and-permanent bases in the Indo-Pacific.[36] In the context of the global geopolitical picture emerging in 2022, however, as the Ukrainian–Russian war continued and worries arose that China could regard it as a precedent for greater aggression in the Indo-Pacific, it seemed to take on more decisive import at least with respect to overall US basing requirements: pulling back US forces on a wholesale basis should not be on the cards in the near future.

Even in calmer times, a major global drawdown would have to be implemented over the course of several US presidential terms, and not abruptly by tweet or démarche, in order to honour commitments to and ensure the safety of allies, and acclimate allies and partners to new American capabilities and long-range modalities for applying them. The US certainly should not commit itself to a foreign policy that is heavy on forward-deployed military power and light on diplomacy, and which does not privilege restraint. Indeed, the Global Posture Review stressed that the US should invariably lead with diplomacy.[37] Vladimir Putin's extreme and seemingly implacable aggression has made the prospect of an easing of tensions between the US and Russia dubious in the short and medium term. But it is conceivable in the other two key strategic regions in the medium to long term. Depending on specific circumstances and operational considerations, Washington could leverage reductions in its forward military presence to encourage the relaxation of tensions. The US should certainly seek an increasingly formidable over-the-horizon surge potential.[38]

In the meantime, paradoxically, a reduction in forward military presence may not always be consistent with a policy that is less focused on military power as a means of achieving stability and security. The devil remains in the situational details.

NOTES

Chapter One

[1] David Vine, 'Lists of US Military Bases Abroad, 1776–2021', American University Digital Research Archive, 4 July 2021, https://doi.org/10.17606/7em4-hb13.

[2] 'US Military Bases Overseas: The Facts', Overseas Base Realignment and Closure Coalition, October 2021, https://www.overseasbases.net/uploads/5/7/1/7/57170837/fact_sheet_on_us_military_bases_overseas_obracc_2021_10_18.pdf.

[3] See, for example, Raphael S. Cohen, 'Why Overseas Military Bases Continue to Make Sense for the United States', *War on the Rocks*, 21 January 2021, https://warontherocks.com/2021/01/why-overseas-military-bases-continue-to-make-sense-for-the-united-states/.

[4] George Washington's Farewell Address, 1796, The Avalon Project, Yale Law School, https://avalon.law.yale.edu/18th_century/washing.asp.

[5] Thomas Jefferson's First Inaugural Address, 1801, The Avalon Project, Yale Law School, https://avalon.law.yale.edu/19th_century/jefinau1.asp.

[6] See James M. McPherson, *Battle Cry of Freedom: The Civil War Era* (Oxford, Oxford University Press), p. 313.

[7] On the strategic evolution of the US summarised here, see George C. Herring, *From Colony to Superpower: US Foreign Relations Since 1776* (Oxford: Oxford University Press, 2011).

[8] Letter from Theodore Roosevelt to Joseph Bucklin Bishop, 23 February 1904, Theodore Roosevelt Center Digital Library, https://www.theodorerooseveltcenter.org/Research/Digital-Library/Record/ImageViewer?libID=o281261&imageNo=1.

[9] See Steven T. Ross, *American War Plans 1890–1939* (London: Frank Cass, 2002).

[10] See Anna Diamond, 'The Original Meanings of the "American Dream" and "America First" Were Starkly Different From How We Use Them Today', *Smithsonian*

Magazine, October 2018, https://www.smithsonianmag.com/history/behold-america-american-dream-slogan-book-sarah-churchwell-180970311/.

11 David Vine, 'The United States Probably Has More Foreign Military Bases Than Any Other People, Nation, or Empire in History', *Nation*, 14 September 2015, https://www.thenation.com/article/world/the-united-states-probably-has-more-foreign-military-bases-than-any-other-people-nation-or-empire-in-history/.

12 See, for example, Townsend Hoopes, 'Overseas Bases in American Strategy', *Foreign Affairs*, vol. 37, no. 1, October 1958, pp. 69–82. See also Harold. W. Rood, 'The Possible Utility of the US Overseas Base Structure', Technical Report no. 34 (Menlo Park, CA: Stanford Research Institute, 1962).

13 Tim Kane, 'The Decline of American Engagement: Patterns in US Troop Deployments', Hoover Institution Economics Working Paper 16101, 11 January 2016, http://www.hoover.org/sites/default/files/research/docs/16101_-_kane_-_decline_of_american_engagement.pdf.

14 See Elliott V. Converse III, *Circling the Earth: United States Plans for a Postwar Overseas Military Base System, 1942–1948* (Maxwell Air Force Base, AL: Air University Press, 2005).

15 David Vine, *Base Nation: How US Military Bases Abroad Harm America and the World* (New York: Metropolitan Books/Henry Holt, 2015).

16 US Department of Defense, *Strengthening US Global Defense Posture* (Washington DC: US Department of Defense, September 2004). See IISS, 'The US Global Posture Review', *Strategic Comments*, vol. 10, no. 7, September 2004.

17 Kane, 'The Decline of American Engagement: Patterns in US Troop Deployments', p. 5.

18 For a prominent example of one touting the notion of an American empire, see Niall Ferguson, *Colossus: The Price of America's Empire* (New York: Penguin Press, 2004). Several ranking American analysts and scholars immediately challenged Ferguson's view; for example, John Lewis Gaddis, 'The Last Empire, for Now', *New York Times*, 25 July 2004, https://www.nytimes.com/2004/07/25/books/the-last-empire-for-now.html.

19 One of the most influential proponents of this idea of US primacy in the early 2000s was Thomas P.M. Barnett, then a senior strategic researcher and professor at the US Naval War College, who developed it in a series of government-sponsored studies and briefings styled 'the Pentagon's new map', and a book of the same name. Thomas P.M. Barnett, *The Pentagon's New Map: War and Peace in the Twenty-first Century* (New York: G.P. Putnam's Sons, 2004). See also Thomas P.M. Barnett, 'The Pentagon's New Map', *Esquire*, March 2003, pp. 174–9, 227–8.

20 Barnett understood the role of the US armed forces after 1991 to be defending and expanding the frontiers of globalisation. Barnett, *The Pentagon's New Map*, pp. 109, 121, 179.

21 *Ibid.*, pp. 379–85.

22 See Alexander Cooley, 'New Bases, Old Politics: The Rise and Decline of the US Military Presence in Central Asia', in Luís Rodrigues and Sergiy Glebov (eds), *Military Bases: Historical Perspectives, Contemporary Challenges*, NATO Science for Peace and Security

Series E: Human and Societal Dynamics, vol. 51 (Amsterdam: IOS Press, 2009), pp. 116–26.

23 See, for example, Akhilesh Pillamarri, 'The United States Just Closed Its Last Base in Central Asia', *Diplomat*, 10 June 2014, https://thediplomat.com/2014/06/the-united-states-just-closed-its-last-base-in-central-asia/.

24 See, for instance, Daniel Benaim and Michael Wahid Hanna, 'The Enduring American Presence in the Middle East', *Foreign Affairs*, 7 August 2019, https://www.foreignaffairs.com/articles/middle-east/2019-08-07/enduring-american-presence-middle-east; and F. Gregory Gause III, 'Should We Stay or Should We Go? The United States and the Middle East', *Survival: Global Politics and Strategy*, vol. 61, no. 5, October–November 2019, pp. 7–24.

25 For a far more detailed and systematic account of the history of the United States overseas defence posture, see Stacie L. Pettyjohn, *U.S. Global Defense Posture, 1783–2011* (Santa Monica, CA: RAND Corporation, 2012).

26 See Alan J. Vick et al., *Air Base Defense: Rethinking Army and Air Force Roles and Functions* (Santa Monica, CA: RAND Corporation, 2020).

27 Vine, 'The United States Probably Has More Foreign Military Bases Than Any Other People, Nation, or Empire in History'.

28 Ellen Mitchell, 'Pentagon Chief Pushes for New Round of Base Closures', *Hill*, 18 October 2017, http://thehill.com/policy/defense/356054-pentagon-chief-pushes-for-new-round-of-base-closures.

29 See Frederico Bartels, 'Report Required: The Pentagon Must Be Pushed into Examining Its Excess Infrastructure', *National Interest*, 8 March 2020, https://nationalinterest.org/feature/report-required-pentagon-must-be-pushed-examining-its-excess-infrastructure-130292; and Aaron Mehtaand Joe Gould, 'The New BRAC Strategy: Capability Over Cost Savings', *Defense News*, 14 December 2017, https://www.defensenews.com/pentagon/2017/12/14/the-new-brac-strategy-capability-over-cost-savings/.

30 Mackenzie Eaglen, 'Esper's Reforms: An Interim Report Card', *Defense One*, 12 October 2020, https://www.defenseone.com/ideas/2020/10/espers-reforms-interim-report-card/169177/.

31 RAND Corporation, *2013 RAND Annual Report*, 2014, https://www.rand.org/pubs/corporate_pubs/CP1-2013.html.

32 James Digby and Joan Goldhamer, 'The Development of Strategic Thinking at RAND, 1948–63: A Mathematical Logician's View – An Interview with Albert Wohlstetter', 5 July 1985 (Santa Monica, CA: RAND Corporation, 1997), p. 35.

33 A.J. Wohlstetter et al., *Selection and Use of Strategic Air Bases*, RAND R-266, 1 April 1954 (declassified 1962), https://www.rand.org/pubs/reports/R0266.html.

34 The RAND study led to the first detailed operational articulation of one of the most fundamental distinctions in nuclear strategy: between first-strike and second-strike deterrence. It was the latter that stabilised the nuclear confrontation and kept the Cold War cold.

35 See Michael J. Lostumbo et al., *Overseas Basing of US Military Forces: An Assessment of Relative Costs and Strategic Benefits* (Santa Monica, CA: RAND Corporation, 2013), https://www.rand.org/pubs/research_reports/RR201.html.

36 See Amy F. Woolf, *Conventional Prompt Global Strike and Long-Range Ballistic Missiles: Background and Issues*, Congressional Research Service, 16 December 2020, https://fas.org/sgp/crs/nuke/R41464.pdf.

37 *Ibid.*

38 See Kingston Reif, 'US Military Debates Ground-launched Missiles', *Arms Control Today*, May 2021, https://www.armscontrol.org/act/2021-05/news/us-military-debates-ground-launched-missiles.

39 See RADM Walter E. Carter, Jr., USN, 'Sea Power in the Precision-missile Age', *Proceedings*, vol. 140, no. 5, May 2014.

40 See, for example, Jerry Hendrix, 'The US Navy Needs to Radically Reassess How It Projects Power', *National Review*, 4 May 2015; Jeff Vandenengel, 'Too Big to Sink', *Proceedings*, vol. 143, no. 5, May 2017; and David W. Wise, 'The US Navy's Big Mistake – Building Tons of Supercarriers', *War Is Boring*, 27 May 2015, https://warisboring.com/the-u-s-navy-s-big-mistake-building-tons-of-supercarriers/. For a contrary view, see Loren B. Thompson, 'Five Reasons US Aircraft Carriers Are Nearly Impossible to Sink', *National Interest*, 11 August 2016, https://nationalinterest.org/blog/the-buzz/five-reasons-us-aircraft-carriers-are-nearly-impossible-sink-17318.

41 See, for example, Loren B. Thompson, 'US Overseas Bases Are Much More Vulnerable Than Aircraft Carriers', *National Interest*, 7 September 2016, http://nationalinterest.org/blog/the-buzz/us-overseas-bases-are-much-more-vulnerable-aircraft-carriers-17612; and Thompson, 'Five Reasons US Aircraft Carriers Are Nearly Impossible to Sink'.

42 See John Glaser, 'The Case Against US Overseas Military Bases', *Foreign Affairs*, 25 July 2017, https://www.foreignaffairs.com/articles/2017-07-25/case-against-us-overseas-military-bases.

43 See Dean Wilkening, 'Hypersonic Weapons and Strategic Stability', *Survival: Global Politics and Strategy*, vol. 61, no. 5, October–November 2019, p. 136.

44 CDR Thomas Shugart, USN, 'First Strike: China's Missile Threat to US Bases in Asia', Center for a New American Security, 28 June 2017, https://www.cnas.org/publications/reports/first-strike-chinas-missile-threat-to-u-s-bases-to-asia.

45 See Daniel Goure, *US Air Dominance in a Fiscally Constrained Environment: Defining Paths to the Future* (Arlington, VA: Lexington Institute, 2013), pp. 26, 33, http://www.lexingtoninstitute.org/wp-content/uploads/2013/09/GlobalPrecisionStrike.pdf.

46 See Joel Wuthnow, *The Impact of Missile Threats on the Reliability of US Overseas Bases: A Framework for Analysis* (Carlisle, PA: US Army War College, Strategic Studies Institute, 2005), available at https://www.jstor.org/stable/resrep11437.

47 Yash Rojas, 'Ellsworth Successfully Validates Base's Long-range Strike Capability', *Pacific Air Forces*, 21 May 2014, http://www.pacaf.af.mil/News/Article-Display/Article/591360/ellsworth-successfully-validates-bases-long-range-strike-capability/.

48 See Wade S. Karren, 'Long-range Strike: The Bedrock of Deterrence and America's Strategic Advantage', *Air & Space Power Journal*, vol. 26, no. 3, May–June 2012, p. 76, http://www.airuniversity.af.mil/Portals/10/ASPJ/

journals/Volume-26_Issue-3/V-Karren.
pdf. See also Mark Gunzinger and Bryan
Clark, *Sustaining America's Precision Strike
Advantage* (Washington DC: Center for
Strategic and Budgetary Assessments,
2015), http://csbaonline.org/uploads/
documents/Sustaining-Americas-
Precision-Strike-Advantage.pdf.

49 See, for example, Jeff Becker, 'When
It Comes to Missiles, Don't Copy
Russia and China – Leapfrog Them',
War on the Rocks, 30 June 2020, https://
warontherocks.com/2020/06/when-
it-comes-to-missiles-dont-copy-
russia-and-china-leapfrog-them/; and
International Institute for Strategic
Studies, 'Chinese and Russian Air-
launched Weapons: A Test for Western
Air Dominance', in *The Military
Balance 2018* (London: Routledge for
the IISS, 2018), pp. 7–9; see also Barry
D. Watts, 'The Evolution of Precision
Strike' (Washington DC: Center for
Strategic and Budgetary Assessments,
2013), http://csbaonline.org/uploads/
documents/Evolution-of-Precision-
Strike-final-v15.pdf.

50 See Dan Gouré, 'Why the US Military
Needs Long Range Precision Fires',
National Interest, 7 October 2020,
https://nationalinterest.org/blog/buzz/
why-us-military-needs-long-range-
precision-fires-170282.

51 Mark Gunzinger, 'Stand In, Standoff',
Air Force Magazine, 1 July 2020, https://
www.airforcemag.com/article/stand-
in-standoff/. See also the longer paper
on which this article is based: Mark
A. Gunzinger, *Long-range Strike:
Resetting the Balance of Stand-in and
Stand-off Forces*, Mitchell Institute for
Aerospace Studies, 18 June 2020, https://
mitchellaerospacepower.org/wp-
content/uploads/2020/06/a2dd91_4f2e5d
f4b4b2464ca6d50d0dcd9ea04f-2.pdf.

52 See Jerry Hendrix, 'Filling the Seams
in US Long-range Penetrating Strike',
Center for a New American Security,
August 2018, https://www.cnas.org/
publications/reports/filling-the-
seams-in-u-s-long-range-penetrating-
strike.

53 See Joseph Trevithick, 'This Is the
Pentagon's $27 Billion Master Plan
to Deter China in the Pacific', *Drive*,
5 March 2021, https://www.thedrive.
com/the-war-zone/39610/this-is-the-
pentagons-27-billion-master-plan-to-
deter-china-in-the-pacific. See also
Jesse Johnson, 'US Indo-Pacific
Chief Suggests Anti-China Missile
Network for Western Pacific', *Japan
Times*, 10 March 2021, https://www.
japantimes.co.jp/news/2021/03/10/
asia-pacific/politics-diplomacy-asia-
pacific/us-china-missile-network/;
and John Gordon IV et al., *Army Fires
Capabilities for 2025 and Beyond* (Santa
Monica, CA: RAND Corporation,
2019), https://www.rand.org/content/
dam/rand/pubs/research_reports/
RR2100/RR2124/RAND_RR2124.pdf.

54 See Steve Trimble, 'Competition for
US Long-range Strike Mission Heats
Up', *Aviation Week*, 26 August 2020,
https://aviationweek.com/defense-
space/missile-defense-weapons/
competition-us-long-range-strike-
mission-heats.

55 See Dan Gouré, 'The Army's "Multi-
domain Operations in 2028" Is an
Important Doctrinal Development',
RealClear Defense, 3 May 2019,
https://www.realcleardefense.com/
articles/2019/05/03/the_armys_multi-
domain_operations_in_2028_is_
an_important_doctrinal_development_
114389.html.

56 Stephanie Worth, 'Sustaining Multi-
domain Operations: The Logistical

Challenges of Future War', Joint Base Elmendorf–Richardson, 11 October 2019, https://www.jber.jb.mil/News/News-Articles/NewsDisplay/Article/1989197/sustaining-multi-domain-operations-the-logistical-challenges-of-future-war/. On the limitations of MDO and the ongoing requirement of massed forces and attrition in war fighting, see Franz-Stefan Gady, 'Manoeuvre Versus Attrition in US Military Operations', *Survival: Global Politics and Strategy*, vol. 63, no. 4, August–September 2021, pp. 131–48.

57 See Ian Williams, 'Adapting to the Hypersonic Era', Center for Strategic and International Studies, 2 November 2020, http://defense360.csis.org/wp-content/uploads/2020/11/Williams_Hypersonic-Era_Final.pdf.

58 See Joseph T. Buontempo and Joseph E. Ringer, 'Airbase Defense Falls Between the Cracks', *Joint Force Quarterly*, no. 97, 2nd Quarter 2020, https://ndupress.ndu.edu/Portals/68/Documents/jfq/jfq-97/jfq-97_114-120_Buontempo-Ringer.pdf.

59 See Michael Beckley, 'In Future Wars, the US Military Will Have Nowhere to Hide', *Foreign Policy*, 20 November 2019, https://foreignpolicy.com/2019/11/20/russia-china-increasingly-able-attack-united-states-bases-networks-war/.

60 See Alan Cummings, 'Hypersonic Weapons: Tactical Uses and Strategic Goals', *War on the Rocks*, 12 November 2019, https://warontherocks.com/2019/11/hypersonic-weapons-tactical-uses-and-strategic-goals/.

61 See Andreas Wenger, 'Crisis and Opportunity: NATO's Transformation and the Multilateralization of Détente, 1966–1968', *Journal of Cold War Studies*, vol. 6, no. 1, Winter 2004, pp. 22–74. France formally reintegrated into NATO's military command structure in 2009.

62 See Jonathan Stevenson, *Thinking Beyond the Unthinkable: Harnessing Doom from the Cold War to the Age of Terror* (New York: Viking, 2008), pp. 51–2.

63 See, for example, Andrew F. Krepinevich, *Maritime Warfare in a Mature Precision-Strike Regime* (Washington DC: Center for Strategic and Budgetary Assessments, 2014), p. 15, https://csbaonline.org/uploads/documents/MMPSR-Web.pdf. See also Frank Hoffman, USMCR, 'What We Can Learn from Jackie Fisher', *Proceedings*, vol. 130, no. 4, April 2004, pp. 68–71.

64 See Stephen Kuper, 'Arsenal Planes Won't Address the US and Allied Long-range Strike Shortfalls', *Defence Connect*, 19 June 2020, https://www.defenceconnect.com.au/strike-air-combat/6305-arsenal-planes-won-t-address-the-us-and-allied-long-range-strike-shortfalls; Abraham Mahsie, '"Not a Moment to Lose": Army in Chase for Long-range Precision Fires', *Washington Examiner*, 24 August 2020, https://www.washingtonexaminer.com/policy/defense-national-security/not-a-moment-to-lose-army-in-chase-for-long-range-precision-fires; and Joseph Trevithick, 'The Army Now Wants Hypersonic Cannons, Loitering Missiles, and a Massive Supergun', *Drive*, 3 April 2018, https://www.thedrive.com/the-war-zone/19847/the-army-now-wants-hypersonic-cannons-loitering-missiles-and-a-massive-supergun. See Shawn Brimley, 'While We Can: Arresting the Erosion of America's Military Edge', Center for a New American Security, December 2015, https://

www.cnas.org/publications/reports/while-we-can-arresting-the-erosion-of-americas-military-edge.

65 Lostumbo et al., 'Overseas Basing of US Military Forces: An Assessment of Relative Costs and Strategic Benefits', pp. 79–80.

66 'US Image Suffers as Publics Around World Question Trump's Leadership', Pew Research Center, 26 June 2017, http://www.pewglobal.org/2017/06/26/u-s-image-suffers-as-publics-around-world-question-trumps-leadership/.

Chapter Two

1 See, for example, Robert Art, *A Grand Strategy for America* (Ithaca, NY: Cornell University Press, 2003); Christopher Layne, 'From Preponderance to Offshore Balancing: America's Future Grand Strategy', *International Security*, vol. 22, no. 1, Summer 1997, pp. 86–124; and Benjamin Schwarz and Christopher Layne, 'A New Grand Strategy', *Atlantic*, January 2002, https://www.theatlantic.com/magazine/archive/2002/01/a-new-grand-strategy/376471/.

2 See, for example, John J. Mearsheimer and Stephen M. Walt, 'The Case for Offshore Balancing', *Foreign Affairs*, vol. 95, no. 4, July–August 2016, pp. 70–83; and Barry Posen, *Restraint: A New Foundation for US Grand Strategy* (Ithaca, NY: Cornell University Press, 2014).

3 See Andrew Bacevich, 'Saving "America First": What Responsible Nationalism Looks Like', *Foreign Affairs*, vol. 96, no. 5, September–October 2017, pp. 57–67.

4 See Elliott Abrams, 'Trump the Traditionalist: A Surprisingly Standard Foreign Policy', *Foreign Affairs*, vol. 96, no. 4, July–August 2017, pp. 10–16.

5 See Michael Crowley, 'Allies and Former US Officials Fear Trump Could Seek NATO Exit in a Second Term', *New York Times*, 3 September 2020, https://www.nytimes.com/2020/09/03/us/politics/trump-nato-withdraw.html.

6 See Jim Garamone, 'Global Posture Review Will Tie Strategy, Defense Policy to Basing', *Defense News*, US Department of Defense, 5 February 2021, https://www.defense.gov/Explore/News/Article/Article/2495328/global-posture-review-will-tie-strategy-defense-policy-to-basing/.

7 Elbridge Colby, 'How to Win America's Next War', *Foreign Policy*, Spring 2019, https://foreignpolicy.com/2019/05/05/how-to-win-americas-next-war-china-russia-military-infrastructure/.

8 See Headquarters, US Department of the Army, 'Army Multi-domain Transformation: Ready to Win in Competition and Conflict', Chief of Staff Paper no. 1 (unclassified version), 16 March 2021, p. 13, https://api.army.mil/e2/c/downloads/2021/03/23/eeac3d01/20210319-csa-paper-1-signed-print-version.pdf.

9 See Steven Simon and Jonathan Stevenson, 'The End of Pax Americana: Why Washington's Middle East

Pullback Makes Sense', *Foreign Affairs*, vol. 94, no. 6, November–December 2015, pp. 2–10.

10 See Simon and Stevenson, 'The End of Pax Americana: Why Washington's Middle East Pullback Makes Sense'.

11 See Richard Burt, 'US Reappraises Persian Gulf Policies', *New York Times*, 1 January 1979, https://www.nytimes.com/1979/01/01/archives/us-reappraises-persian-gulf-policies-steps-to-bolster-confidence.html.

12 See State of the Union Address 1980, speech delivered by Jimmy Carter, Jimmy Carter Presidential Library and Museum, 23 January 1980, https://www.jimmycarterlibrary.gov/assets/documents/speeches/su80jec.phtml.

13 See, for example, Adam Taylor, 'As Trump Tries to End "Endless Wars," America's Biggest Mideast Base Is Getting Bigger', *Washington Post*, 21 August 2019, https://www.washingtonpost.com/world/as-trump-tries-to-end-endless-wars-americas-biggest-mideast-base-is-getting-bigger/2019/08/20/47ac5854-bab4-11e9-8e83-4e6687e99814_story.html.

14 See Joyce Karam and Mustafa Alrawi, 'Centcom: Qatar Dispute Hindering Long-term Planning at Udeid Airbase', *National*, 29 July 2017, https://www.thenationalnews.com/world/the-americas/centcom-qatar-dispute-hindering-long-term-planning-at-udeid-airbase-1.615046.

15 CAOC Fact Sheet, 'US Air Forces Central Command', 1 July 2017, http://www.afcent.af.mil/About/Fact-Sheets/Display/Article/217803/combined-air-operations-center-caoc/.

16 See David Des Roches, 'A Base Is More Than Buildings: The Military Implications of the Qatar Crisis', *War on the Rocks*, 8 June 2017, https://warontherocks.com/2017/06/a-base-is-more-than-buildings-the-military-implications-of-the-qatar-crisis/.

17 F. Gregory Gause III, 'Should We Stay or Should We Go? The United States and the Middle East', *Survival: Global Politics and Strategy*, vol. 61, no. 5, October–November 2019, pp. 7–24.

18 See Michael R. Auslin, 'The Question of American Strategy in the Indo-Pacific', Hoover Institution Essay on a US Strategic Vision in a Changing World, Hoover Institute, 2018, p. 5, https://www.hoover.org/sites/default/files/research/docs/auslin_webreadypdf.pdf.

19 *Ibid.*, pp. 5–6.

20 'US Security Strategy for the East Asia-Pacific Region', US Department of Defense, February 1995, https://apps.dtic.mil/sti/citations/ADA298441.

21 United Nations Conference on Trade and Development, 'Review of Maritime Transport 2021', United Nations, 2021, https://unctad.org/system/files/official-document/rmt2021_en_0.pdf.

22 For a particularly sobering view of China's rise and its geopolitical implications, see John J. Mearsheimer, 'The Gathering Storm: China's Challenge to US Power in Asia', *Chinese Journal of International Politics*, vol. 3, no. 4, December 2010, pp. 381–96. For a balanced and nicely contextualised assessment of China's growing maritime capabilities, see Andrew J. Erickson, 'Rising Tide, Dispersing Waves: Opportunities and Challenges for China's Seapower Development', *Journal of Strategic Studies*, vol. 37, no. 3, April 2014, pp. 372–402.

23 On the evolution and character of this new model, see Daniel Tobin,

'How Xi Jinping's "New Era" Should Have Ended US Debate on Beijing's Ambitions', Center for Strategic and International Studies, 8 May 2020, https://www.csis.org/analysis/how-xi-jinpings-new-era-should-have-ended-us-debate-beijings-ambitions.

24 See Brendan Taylor, *Dangerous Decade: Taiwan's Security and Crisis Management*, Adelphi 470–1 (Abingdon: Routledge for the IISS, 2019).

25 See Jacob Mardell, 'The "Community of Common Destiny" in Xi Jinping's New Era', *Diplomat*, 25 October 2017, https://thediplomat.com/2017/10/the-community-of-common-destiny-in-xi-jinpings-new-era/.

26 See Dan Olmstead, 'WWII Polls: Should the United States Keep Troops in Germany?', National WWII Museum, New Orleans, LA, https://www.nationalww2museum.org/war/articles/should-united-states-keep-troops-germany.

27 See Dana H. Allin, *NATO's Balkan Interventions*, Adelphi 347 (London: Oxford University Press for the International Institute for Strategic Studies, 2002).

28 See, for example, Julian E. Barnes and Helene Cooper, 'Trump Discussed Pulling US From NATO, Aides Say Amid New Concerns Over Russia', *New York Times*, 14 January 2019, https://www.nytimes.com/2019/01/14/us/politics/nato-president-trump.html.

29 James Stavridis, 'Why NATO Is Essential for World Peace, According to Its Former Commander', *Time*, 4 April 2019, https://time.com/5564171/why-nato-is-essential-world-peace/.

30 See Michael A. Allen, Carla Martinez Machain and Michael E. Flynn, 'The US Military Presence in Europe Has Been Declining for 30 Years – the Current Crisis in Ukraine May Reverse That Trend', *Conversation*, 25 January 2022, https://theconversation.com/the-us-military-presence-in-europe-has-been-declining-for-30-years-the-current-crisis-in-ukraine-may-reverse-that-trend-175595.

31 US Department of Defense, 'DoD Announces European Infrastructure Consolidation Actions and F-35 Basing in Europe', 8 January 2015, https://www.defense.gov/News/News-Releases/News-Release-View/Article/605338/; and Tony Osborne, 'USAF Names RAF Lakenheath as F-35A Base, Unveils Closures', *Aerospace Daily & Defense Report*, 8 January 2015, http://aviationweek.com/defense/usaf-names-raf-lakenheath-f-35a-base-unveils-closures.

32 Philip M. Breedlove, 'NATO's Next Act: How to Handle Russia and Other Threats', *Foreign Affairs*, vol. 95, no. 4, July–August 2016, pp. 96–105.

33 See Luke Coffey, 'Keeping America Safe: Why US Bases in Europe Remain Vital', Heritage Foundation, 11 July 2012, http://www.heritage.org/defense/report/keeping-america-safe-why-us-bases-europe-remain-vital.

34 See Douglas Barrie et al., *Defending Europe: Scenario-based Capability Requirements for NATO's European Members*, International Institute for Strategic Studies, April 2019, https://www.iiss.org/blogs/research-paper/2019/05/defending-europe. For a critique of this analysis, see Barry R. Posen, 'Europe Can Defend Itself', *Survival: Global Politics and Strategy*, vol. 62, no. 6, December 2020–January 2021, pp. 7–34. For replies to this critique from the authors of the original study and other experts, see

'Forum: Can Europe Defend Itself', *Survival: Global Politics and Strategy*, vol. 63, no. 1, February–March 2021, pp. 17–49.

35 'Statement of General Curtis M. Scararrotti, Commander, United States European Command, 23 March 2017', Senate Armed Services Committee, https://www.armed-services.senate.gov/imo/media/doc/Scaparrotti_03-23-17.pdf; and 2017 HASC Opening Statement and Full Statement as Delivered by General Curtis Scaparrotti, 28 March 2017, https://www.eucom.mil/transcript/35614/2017-hasc-opening-statement-and-full-transcript-as-delivered-by-general-curtis-scaparrotti.

36 Wales Summit Declaration, 5 September 2014, NATO, https://www.nato.int/cps/en/natohq/official_texts_112964.htm.

37 See Lucie Béraud-Sudreau and Bastian Giegerich, 'NATO Defence Spending and European Threat Perceptions', *Survival: Global Politics and Strategy*, vol. 60, no. 4, August–September 2018, pp. 53–74.

38 *Ibid.*, p. 59.

39 International Institute for Strategic Studies, *The Military Balance 2021* (London: Routledge for the IISS, 2021), p. 73.

40 See International Institute for Strategic Studies, *The Military Balance 2017* (London: Routledge for the IISS, 2017), pp. 71–4.

41 Barrie et al., *Defending Europe: Scenario-based Capability Requirements for NATO's European Members*.

42 Elbridge Colby and Jonathan Solomon, 'Facing Russia: Conventional Defence and Deterrence in Europe', *Survival: Global Politics and Strategy*, vol. 57, no. 6, December 2015–January 2016,

p. 27. See also International Institute for Strategic Studies, *Russia's Military Modernisation: An Assessment*, IISS Strategic Dossier (London: Routledge for the IISS, 2020).

43 *Ibid.*, pp. 28–31.

44 'NATO's Continuing Adaptation', *Strategic Comments*, IISS, vol. 23, no. 22, 5 July 2017.

45 See 'Exercise Brilliant Jump II Closes With Success', Supreme Headquarters Allied Powers Europe, NATO, 10 November 2020, https://shape.nato.int/news-archive/2020/exercise-brilliant-jump-ii-2020-closes-with-success.

46 See Fabrice Pothier, 'An Area Access Strategy for NATO', *Survival: Global Politics and Strategy*, vol. 59, no. 3, June–July 2017, pp. 73–9.

47 Martin Zapfe, 'Deterrence from the Ground Up: Understanding NATO's Enhanced Forward Presence', *Survival: Global Politics and Strategy*, vol. 59, no. 3, June–July 2017, pp. 152–7.

48 See Colby and Solomon, 'Facing Russia: Conventional Defence and Deterrence in Europe'.

49 See Jeffrey Engel, '"Over There … to Stay This Time": The Forward-deployment of American Basing Strategy in the Cold War and Beyond', in Luís Rodrigues and Sergiy Glebov (eds), *Military Bases: Historical Perspectives, Contemporary Challenges*, NATO Science for Peace and Security Series E: Human and Societal Dynamics, vol. 51 (Amsterdam: IOS Press, 2009), pp. 17–28.

50 See, for example, Geoffrey F. Gresh, *Gulf Security and the US Military: Regime Survival and the Politics of Basing* (Stanford, CA: Stanford University Press, 2015); Amy Austin Holmes, *Social Unrest and American Military Bases in Turkey and Germany Since 1945*

(Cambridge: Cambridge University Press, 2014); Yuko Kawato, *Protests Against US Military Base Policy in Asia: Persuasion and Its Limits* (Stanford, CA: Stanford University Press, 2015); and David Vine, *Base Nation: How US Military Bases Abroad Harm America and the World* (New York: Metropolitan Books/Henry Holt, 2015). See also David Vine, 'The Pentagon's New Base Plan Will Achieve the Exact Opposite of Its Goal', *Nation*, 14 January 2016, https://www.thenation.com/article/the-pentagons-new-base-plan-will-achieve-the-exact-opposite-of-its-goal/; and Andrew I. Yeo, 'The Politics of Overseas Military Bases', *Perspectives on Politics*, vol. 15, no. 1, March 2017, pp. 129–36 (review essay).

Chapter Three

1   IISS Military Balance+ database, https://milbalplus.iiss.org, accessed April 2022.

2   See Bruce Riedel and Michael E. O'Hanlon, 'How to Downsize the US Presence in the Middle East', Brookings Institution, 20 October 2020, https://www.brookings.edu/blog/order-from-chaos/2020/10/20/how-to-downsize-the-us-presence-in-the-middle-east/. More enthusiastic proponents of offshore balancing have advocated 'no large sustained or permanent US military presence in the region'; see Emma Ashford, 'Unbalanced: Rethinking America's Commitment to the Middle East', *Strategic Studies Quarterly*, vol. 12, no. 1, Spring 2018, p. 144. More radical proposals have also surfaced; see also Mike Sweeney, 'A Plan for US Withdrawal from the Middle East', Defense Priorities, 21 December 2020, https://www.defensepriorities.org/explainers/a-plan-for-us-withdrawal-from-the-middle-east.

3   See David Des Roches, 'A Base Is More Than Buildings: The Military Implications of the Qatar Crisis', *War on the Rocks*, 8 June 2017, https://warontherocks.com/2017/06/a-base-is-more-than-buildings-the-military-implications-of-the-qatar-crisis/.

4   Jeremy Diamond, 'Could Military Force Still Be Used Against Iran?', *CNN Politics*, 2 April 2015, http://www.cnn.com/2015/04/02/politics/iran-nuclear-deal-military-attack/.

5   See, for example, Dov S. Zakheim, 'The Military Option', *Iran Primer*, United States Institute of Peace, http://iranprimer.usip.org/resource/military-option. On the pitfalls of the military option, see Patrick Clawson and Michael Eisenstadt, 'Halting Iran's Nuclear Programme: The Military Option', *Survival: Global Politics and Strategy*, vol. 50, no. 5, October–November 2008, pp. 13–19.

6   See, for example, Mahsa Rouhi, 'US–Iran Tensions and the Oil Factor', *Survival: Global Politics and Strategy*, vol. 60, no. 5, October–November 2018, pp. 33–40. For data on transit volumes through the straits, see US Energy Information Administration, 'The Strait of Hormuz Is the World's Most Important Oil Transit

Chokepoint', 20 June 2019, https://www.eia.gov/todayinenergy/detail.php?id=39932; and US Energy Information Administration, 'The Bab el-Mandeb Strait Is a Strategic Route for Oil and Natural Gas Shipments', 27 August 2019, https://www.eia.gov/todayinenergy/detail.php?id=41073.

7 Arash Karami, 'IRGC: Naval Exercise Also "Media-Psychological" Operation', *Al-Monitor*, 2 March 2015, http://www.al-monitor.com/pulse/ru/contents/articles/originals/2015/03/iran-naval-exercise-us-aircraft-carrier.html; and Thomas Erdbrink, 'Iran's Navy Blasts Away at a Mock US Carrier', *New York Times*, 25 February 2015, https://www.nytimes.com/2015/02/26/world/middleeast/in-mock-attack-iranian-navy-blasts-away-at-replica-us-aircraft-carrier.html.

8 On the escalatory dangers of a US–Iran confrontation over the Strait of Hormuz, see Caitlin Talmadge, 'Closing Time: Assessing the Iranian Threat to the Strait of Hormuz', *International Security*, vol. 33, no. 1, Summer 2008, pp. 82–117.

9 See Rick Gladstone, 'Strait of Hormuz Once Again at Center of US–Iran Strife', *New York Times*, 1 May 2015, http://www.nytimes.com/2015/05/02/world/middleeast/strait-of-hormuz-once-again-at-center-of-us-iran-strife.html.

10 See Jim Sciutto and Jamie Crawford, 'US: Warships Near Yemen Create "Options" for Dealing with Iranian Vessels', *CNN News*, 22 April 2015, http://www.cnn.com/2015/04/20/politics/iran-united-states-warships-monitoring/.

11 Gina Harkins, 'Navy Sends Nuclear Sub to Strait of Hormuz as Anniversary of Soleimani Killing Approaches', *Military.com*, 21 December 2020, https://www.military.com/daily-news/2020/12/21/navy-sends-nuclear-sub-strait-of-hormuz-anniversary-of-soleimani-killing-approaches.html.

12 See Howard Fineman, 'US Plans to Inch Up Role in Syria', *Huffington Post*, 21 February 2014, http://www.huffingtonpost.com/2014/02/21/us-syria-aid_n_4827166.html.

13 On the challenges of establishing and maintaining a no-fly zone, see, for example, Clint Hinote, 'Everything You Need to Know About No-Fly Zones', *Defense One*, 5 May 2015, http://www.defenseone.com/ideas/2015/05/everything-you-need-know-about-no-fly-zones/111898/; and Karl Mueller, 'Is a No-fly Zone Over Syria Achievable?', *Newsweek*, 18 October 2015, http://www.newsweek.com/no-fly-zone-over-syria-achievable-384171.

14 See Sam LaGrone, 'Fifth US Destroyer Moves Closer to Syria', *USNI News*, 30 August 2013, http://news.usni.org/2013/08/30/fifth-u-s-destroyer-moves-closer-syria.

15 See 'Department of Defense Press Briefing by Pentagon Chief Spokesperson Dana W. White and Joint Staff Director Lt. Gen. Kenneth F. McKenzie Jr. in the Pentagon Briefing Room', US Department of Defense, 14 April 2018, https://www.defense.gov/News/Transcripts/Transcript/Article/1493749/?department-of-defense-press-briefing-by-pentagon-chief-spokesperson-dana-w-whit.

16 See David D. Kirkpatrick, 'SEAL Team Raids a Tanker and Thwarts a Militia's Bid to Sell Libyan Oil', *New York Times*, 17 March 2014, http://www.nytimes.com/2014/03/18/world/middleeast/libya-oil-tanker.html?_r=0.

17 Helene Cooper and Eric Schmitt,

'US Strikes Help Libyan Forces Against ISIS in Surt', *New York Times*, 2 August 2016, https://www.nytimes.com/2016/08/03/us/politics/drone-airstrikes-libya-isis.html; and Adam Entous and Missy Ryan, 'US Has Secretly Expanded Its Global Network of Drone Bases to North Africa', *Washington Post*, 26 October 2016, https://www.washingtonpost.com/world/national-security/us-has-secretly-expanded-its-global-network-of-drone-bases-to-north-africa/2016/10/26/ff19633c-9b7d-11e6-9980-50913d68eacb_story.html.

18 See J.P. Lawrence, 'US Military Shifts Army Basing from Qatar to Jordan in Move That Could Provide Leverage Against Iran', *Stars and Stripes*, 1 July 2021, https://www.stripes.com/branches/army/2021-07-01/us-military-closes-qatar-camps-in-move-that-could-play-into-iran-policy-2009140.html.

19 See Eli Lake, 'Israel Could Get Dragged Into ISIS's War, Obama Admin Warns', *Daily Beast*, 27 June 2014, http://www.thedailybeast.com/articles/2014/06/27/israel-could-get-dragged-into-isis-s-war-obama-admin-warns.html.

20 For a good account of the logistics and procedures involved in a FAST deployment, see Tyler Rogoway, 'How the Marines Could Evacuate the US Embassy in Libya', *Foxtrot Alpha*, 23 May 2014, http://foxtrotalpha.jalopnik.com/how-the-marines-could-evacuate-the-u-s-embassy-in-liby-1580532779.

21 See Kenneth Katzman, 'Qatar: Governance, Security, and US Policy', Congressional Research Service, 1 September 2017, https://fas.org/sgp/crs/mideast/R44533.pdf.

22 Courtney Kube, 'US Military Has Begun Reestablishing Air Base Inside Saudi Arabia', NBC, 19 July 2019, https://www.nbcnews.com/news/mideast/u-s-military-has-begun-reestablishing-air-base-inside-saudi-n1031916. The *Patriot*s were withdrawn in September 2021.

23 See, for example, Hedrick Simoes, 'Bahrain Expansion Latest Signal of Continued US Presence', *Stars and Stripes*, 13 December 2013, https://www.stripes.com/news/bahrain-expansion-latest-signal-of-continued-us-presence-1.257371.

24 See Richard McDaniel, 'No "Plan B": US Strategic Access in the Middle East and the Question of Bahrain', Federal Executive Fellow Policy Paper 15, Brookings Institution, 24 June 2013, pp. 18–19, http://www.brookings.edu/research/papers/2013/06/24-us-strategic-access-middle-east-bahrain-mcdaniel.

25 See Julian Pecquet, 'Bahrain Bristles as US Threatens to Move Fleet', *US News & World Report*, 19 May 2015, http://www.usnews.com/news/articles/2015/05/19/bahrain-bristles-at-threat-to-move-5th-fleet.

26 See 'US, Israel, UAE, Bahrain Launch Joint Naval Drills in Red Sea', Al-Jazeera, 11 November 2021, https://www.aljazeera.com/news/2021/11/11/us-israel-uae-bahrain-launch-joint-naval-drills-in-red-sea.

27 On the historical, legal, political and operational niceties of base access, see Stacie L. Pettyjohn and Jennifer Kavanagh, *Access Granted: Political Challenges to the U.S. Overseas Military Presence, 1945–2014* (Santa Monica, CA: RAND Corporation, 2016).

28 See McDaniel, 'No "Plan B": US Strategic Access in the Middle East

and the Question of Bahrain'.

29 See Michael McDevitt, 'America's Interest in Diego Garcia', *War on the Rocks*, 3 June 2020, https://warontherocks.com/2020/06/americas-interest-in-diego-garcia/.

30 Christopher P. Cavas, 'Interview: Vice Adm. John Miller', *Defense News*, 3 March 2015, https://www.defensenews.com/naval/2015/03/03/interview-vice-adm-john-miller/.

31 See 'Montrose Resumes Middle East Mission After Complex Engineering Job', Royal Navy, 22 June 2021, https://www.royalnavy.mod.uk/news-and-latest-activity/news/2021/june/22/20210622-montrose-duqm.

32 See 'Ships of the Eisenhower Carrier Strike Group Conduct Port Visit in Duqm', *America's Navy*, 12 April 2021, https://www.navy.mil/Press-Office/News-Stories/Article/2568663/ships-of-the-eisenhower-carrier-strike-group-conduct-port-visit-in-duqm/.

33 See George Cafiero and Theodore Karasik, 'Can Oman's Stability Outlive Sultan Qaboos?', Middle East Institute, 27 April 2016, https://www.mei.edu/content/can-oman-stability-outlive-sultan-qaboos; and James Fromson and Steven Simon, 'Visions of Omani Reform', *Survival: Global Politics and Strategy*, vol. 61, no. 4, August–September 2019, pp. 99–116.

34 See Brus E. Vidal, 'Command and Control of AFCENT from Shaw, Not CAOC', US Central Command, 1 October 2019, https://www.centcom.mil/MEDIA/NEWS-ARTICLES/News-Article-View/Article/1976249/command-and-control-of-afcent-from-shaw-not-caoc/.

35 See McDaniel, 'No "Plan B": US Strategic Access in the Middle East and the Question of Bahrain', pp. 21–2.

36 See Kris Osborn, 'Why the US Navy Is Building Another Huge, Mobile Sea Base', *National Interest*, 30 June 2020, https://nationalinterest.org/blog/buzz/why-us-navy-building-another-huge-mobile-sea-base-163789.

37 See 'USS Lewis B. Puller Credited with Saving Lives of Rescued Mariners', *America's Navy*, 9 January 2022, https://www.navy.mil/Press-Office/News-Stories/Article/2893376/uss-lewis-b-puller-credited-with-saving-lives-of-rescued-mariners/.

38 McDaniel, 'No "Plan B": US Strategic Access in the Middle East and the Question of Bahrain', p. 19.

39 *Ibid.*, p. 25.

40 *Ibid.*, pp. 19–22.

41 See 'Iranian Ships Moving Away from Yemen: US Official', Reuters, 23 April 2015, https://www.reuters.com/article/us-yemen-security-ships-idUSKBN0NE23920150423.

42 See Ryan T. Newell, 'Assessing the US Aircraft Carrier Gap in the Gulf', *Policy Watch 2497*, Washington Institute for Near East Policy, 5 October 2015, http://www.washingtoninstitute.org/policy-analysis/view/assessing-the-u.s.-aircraft-carrier-gap-in-the-gulf.

43 See, for example, 'Department of Defense Press Briefing by Lt. Gen. Mayville in the Pentagon Briefing Room', US Department of Defense, 11 August 2014, https://www.defense.gov/News/Transcripts/Transcript/Article/606909/department-of-defense-press-briefing-by-lt-gen-mayville-in-the-pentagon-briefin/; Joe Pappalardo, 'Year One: Inside the Air War Against ISIS', *Popular Mechanics*, 21 September 2015, https://www.popularmechanics.com/military/a17383/year-one-inside-the-air-war-

against-isis/; Benjamin W. Stratton, 'Misawa Pilots Save Iraqi Civilians, Earn 2014 Mackay Trophy', *Air Force*, 15 December 2015, https://www.af.mil/News/Article-Display/Article/634210/misawa-pilots-save-iraqi-civilians-earn-2014-mackay-trophy/; and Becca Wasser et al., 'The Role of US Airpower in Defeating ISIS', RAND Corporation, 2021, https://www.rand.org/pubs/research_briefs/RBA388-1.html.

44 Richard Sisk, 'US Navy Down to Five Aircraft Carriers at Sea, None in the Mideast', *Military.com*, 4 November 2015, http://www.military.com/daily-news/2015/11/04/us-navy-down-to-five-aircraft-carriers-at-sea-none-the-mideast.html.

45 Other air assets included land-based F-16s out of Incirlik Air Base in Turkey. But the Air Force's ability to use Incirlik for air-combat operations remains uncertain due to ongoing political tension between the US and Turkey. If Washington is inclined to maintain the tenuous status quo between the two countries (as its hesitancy about removing B-61 tactical nuclear bombs from Turkey suggests) it would be reluctant to strain bilateral relations by running actual military operations out of Incirlik. See John Vandiver, 'US Reviewing Plans to Move Nuclear Weapons from Incirlik, Report Says', *Stars and Stripes*, 15 October 2019, https://www.stripes.com/news/us-reviewing-plans-to-move-nuclear-weapons-from-incirlik-report-says-1.603116.

46 Megan Eckstein, 'GAO: Rampant Maintenance Delays Caused by Contracting, Workforce Issues', *USNI News*, 3 May 2016, https://news.usni.org/2016/05/03/gao-rampant-maintenance-delays-caused-by-contracting-workforce-issues. See also Seth Cropsey, *Seablindness: How Political Neglect Is Choking American Seapower and What to Do About It* (New York: Encounter Books, 2017).

47 Newell, 'Assessing the US Aircraft Carrier Gap in the Gulf'.

48 See Demetri Sevastopulo, 'Russian Navy Presents US with Fresh Challenge', *Financial Times*, 2 November 2015, http://www.ft.com/cms/s/0/47314ece-80a8-11e5-8095-ed1a37d1e096.html#axzz3sR8odRUZ.

49 See Robert Farley, 'America's Aircraft Carrier Gap', *Diplomat*, 10 July 2015, http://thediplomat.com/2015/07/americas-aircraft-carrier-challenge/.

50 See Carl Prine, 'Navy Struggles with Shortage of Aircraft Carriers', *San Diego Union-Tribune*, 23 June 2017, http://www.sandiegouniontribune.com/military/sd-me-carrier-gap-20170623-story.html.

51 Jeta Pillai, 'Naval Dockyard, UK Firm in Tieup', *Oman Tribune*, 21 March 2017, https://web.archive.org/web/20170321220955/http://omantribune.com/details/32946/.

52 US Navy Press Release, 'USS *Truxtun* Visits Duqm, Oman', US Navy News Service, 19 April 2017, https://www.navy.mil/Press-Office/News-Stories/Article/2255611/uss-truxtun-visits-duqm-oman/.

53 See 'US Security Cooperation with Oman – Fact Sheet', Bureau of Political-Military Affairs, US Department of State, 15 June 2021, https://www.state.gov/u-s-security-cooperation-with-oman/.

54 See, for example, Russ Read, 'Iran's Missile Attack on ISIS Was Coordinated with Assad, Went Through Iraqi Airspace',

National Interest, 19 June 2017, http://nationalinterest.org/blog/the-buzz/irans-missile-attack-isis-was-coordinated-assad-went-through-21222; and 'Iran IRGC Fires Six Zolfaqar MRV Missiles to ISIS Terrorists Bases in Dayr al-Zawr Syria', YouTube, 19 June 2017, https://www.youtube.com/watch?v=Xdm4UNgwtIQ.

55   See, for example, Jon Gambrell, 'Iran Missiles Target Fake Carrier as US Bases Go on Alert', Associated Press, 28 July 2020, https://apnews.com/article/strait-of-hormuz-dubai-ap-top-news-iran-united-arab-emirates-b931ea8d6751c953233665202a59e5e1; Tyler Rogoway, 'Iran's Missiles Landing Within 100 Miles of a US Carrier Is Provocative but Not Much Else', *Drive*, 17 January 2021, https://www.

thedrive.com/the-war-zone/38773/irans-missiles-landing-within-100-miles-of-a-u-s-carrier-group-is-provocative-but-not-much-else; and Loren Thompson, 'Claims of Aircraft Carrier Vulnerability Are False, but the Versatility Is Real', *Forbes*, 9 June 2020, https://www.forbes.com/sites/lorenthompson/2020/06/09/claims-of-aircraft-carrier-vulnerability-are-false-but-the-versatility-is-real/?sh=7397acda591a. For the standard confident view, see 'Aircraft Carrier (In)Vulnerability: What It Takes to Successfully Attack an American Aircraft Carrier', Naval Strike Forum, Lexington Institute, 2001, https://www.lexingtoninstitute.org/wp-content/uploads/aircraft-carrier-invulnerability.pdf.

Chapter Four

1   Over the last several years, reports have emerged of classified wargames in which the US loses to China in various regional contingencies. These have been designed and executed by highly capable and responsible analysts and cannot be dismissed. See, for example, Kathy Gilsinan, 'How the US Could Lose a War with China', *Atlantic*, 25 July 2019, https://www.theatlantic.com/politics/archive/2019/07/china-us-war/594793/; James Kitfield, '"We're Going to Lose Fast": US Air Force Held a War Game That Started with a Chinese Biological Attack', Yahoo! News, 10 March 2021, https://www.yahoo.com/now/were-going-to-lose-fast-us-air-force-held-a-war-game-that-started-with-a-chinese-biological-

attack-170003936.html; and Kyle Mizokami, 'A 2013 Wargame Proves the US Navy Could Lose a South China Sea War', *National Interest*, 25 December 2020, https://nationalinterest.org/blog/reboot/2013-wargame-proves-us-navy-could-lose-south-china-sea-war-175198. But advocates of increased defence spending may spin the results pessimistically to win funding, and there are some unknowns that wargames cannot simulate – such as China's relative war-fighting inexperience – that could favour the US.

2   On China's preoccupation with control and its overall challenge, see David C. Gompert, 'Four Circles: Comprehending the China

Challenge', *Survival: Global Politics and Strategy*, vol. 64, no. 2, April–May 2022, pp. 95–110.

3   See Office of the Under Secretary of Defense (Comptroller), 'Pacific Deterrence Initiative', US Department of Defense, May 2021, https://comptroller.defense.gov/Portals/45/Documents/defbudget/FY2022/fy2022_Pacific_Deterrence_Initiative.pdf. See also Elbridge Colby and Walter Slocombe, 'The State of (Deterrence by) Denial', *War on the Rocks*, 22 March 2021, https://warontherocks.com/2021/03/the-state-of-deterrence-by-denial/.

4   Gen. David H. Berger, Commandant of the Marine Corps, 'Force Design 2030', Department of the Navy, United States Marine Corps, March 2020, https://www.hqmc.marines.mil/Portals/142/Docs/CMC38 Force Design 2030 Report Phase I and II.pdf?ver=2020-03-26-121328-460

5   See, for example, Megan Eckstein, 'Marines' Force Design 2030 May Allow MEUs Tailored for Different Geographies, Adversaries', *USNI News*, 2 April 2020, https://news.usni.org/2020/04/02/marines-force-design-2030-may-allow-meus-tailored-for-different-geographies-adversaries; and Benjamin Jensen, 'The Rest of the Story: Evaluating the US Marine Corps Force Design 2030', *War on the Rocks*, 27 April 2020, https://warontherocks.com/2020/04/the-rest-of-the-story-evaluating-the-u-s-marine-corps-force-design-2030/.

6   See, respectively, 'MGM-140 Army Tactical Missile System (ATACMS)', Missile Threat, CSIS Missile Defense Project, updated as of 31 July 2021, https://missilethreat.csis.org/missile/atacms/; Andrew Eversden,

'The Army Could Get Its Next-gen Precision Strike Missiles in FY27', *Breaking Defense*, 3 May 2022, https://breakingdefense.com/2022/05/the-army-could-get-its-next-gen-precision-strike-missiles-in-fy27/; Michael Peck, 'Will the Philippines Purchase HIMARS to Counter China?', *National Interest*, 6 September 2021, https://nationalinterest.org/blog/reboot/will-philippines-purchase-himars-counter-china-192901; and Thomas Shugart, 'The US Army's Long-range Missiles Could Be the Perfect Tool to Neutralize China's Artificial Islands', *National Interest*, 10 November 2016, http://nationalinterest.org/blog/the-buzz/the-us-armys-long-range-missiles-could-be-the-perfect-tool-18357.

7   See Sydney J. Freedburg Jr, '"$64K Question": Where in Pacific Do Army Missiles Go?', *Breaking Defense*, 16 March 2021, https://breakingdefense.com/2021/03/64k-question-where-in-pacific-do-army-missiles-go/.

8   David H. Berger, 'Force Design 2030', Department of the Navy, United States Marine Corps, March 2020, p. 3, https://www.hqmc.marines.mil/Portals/142/Docs/CMC38 Force Design 2030 Report Phase I and II.pdf?ver=2020-03-26-121328-460. See also, for example, Gidget Fuentes, 'Marines Fire HIMARS from Ship in Sea Control Experiment with Navy', *USNI News*, 24 October 2017, https://news.usni.org/2017/10/24/marines-fire-himars-ship-sea-control-experiment-navy; and Joseph Trevithick, 'HiMARS Goes to Sea: US Marines Now Fire Guided Artillery Rockets from Ships', *Drive*, 24 October 2017, https://www.thedrive.com/the-war-zone/15410/himars-goes-to-sea-us-marines-now-fire-guided-

artillery-rockets-from-ships.

9   Mark Gunzinger and Bryan Clark, 'Sustaining America's Precision Strike Advantage', Center for Strategic and Budgetary Assessments, 2015, pp. 31–4, https://csbaonline.org/uploads/documents/Sustaining-Americas-Precision-Strike-Advantage.pdf. A dearth of airborne-refuelling resources for American reconnaissance aircraft does make forward basing for such aircraft very useful in peacetime. But given that only about a dozen planes would have to be simultaneously aloft at any given time, intelligence, surveillance and reconnaissance needs would not warrant an extensive permanent-basing presence and could be met in a pinch by carriers. Furthermore, long-dwelling drones along with airborne-refuelling resources currently in procurement for the P-8 *Poseidon* patrol aircraft should ease the need for forward basing in the medium term, though endurance will remain a challenge.

10   See Michael W. Pietrucha, 'Making Places, Not Bases a Reality', *Proceedings*, vol. 141, no. 10, October 2015, pp. 54–9, https://www.usni.org/magazines/proceedings/2015/october/making-places-not-bases-reality.

11   Wyatt Olsen, 'Pacific Air Forces Commander Stresses a More Diverse, Expeditionary-styled Fleet', *Stars and Stripes*, 4 September 2019, https://www.stripes.com/news/pacific/pacific-air-forces-commander-stresses-a-more-dispersed-expeditionary-style-fleet-1.597169.

12   See Sam J. Tangredi, 'The Role of Sea Basing', in Carnes Lord and Andrew Erickson (eds), *Rebalancing US Forces: Basing and Forward Presence in the Indo-Pacific* (Annapolis, MD: Naval Institute Press, 2014), pp. 199–212.

13   See Ian Easton, 'China's Evolving Reconnaissance-strike Capabilities: Implications for the US–Japan Alliance', Project 2049 Institute, The Japan Institute of International Affairs, February 2014, p. 6, https://project2049.net/wp-content/uploads/2018/06/Chinas_Evolving_Reconnaissance_Strike_Capabilities_Easton.pdf.

14   Jordan Wilson, 'China's Expanding Ability to Conduct Conventional Missile Strikes on Guam', Center for International Maritime Security, 16 August 2016, http://cimsec.org/chinas-expanding-ability-conduct-conventional-missile-strikes-guam/27099; Thomas Gibbons-Neff, 'Chinese Ballistic Missiles Dubbed "Guam Killer" Pose Increasing Threat to US Island, Report Says', *Washington Post*, 11 May 2016, https://www.washingtonpost.com/news/checkpoint/wp/2016/05/11/chinese-ballistic-missiles-dubbed-guam-killer-pose-increasing-threat-to-u-s-island-report-says/; and Keith Johnson, 'China's "Guam Killers" Threaten US Anchor Base in the Pacific', *Foreign Policy*, 11 May 2016, http://foreignpolicy.com/2016/05/11/chinas-guam-killers-threaten-u-s-anchor-base-in-pacific/.

15   Choe Sang-Hun and David E. Sanger, 'North Korea Fires Missile Over Japan', *New York Times*, 28 August 2017, https://www.nytimes.com/2017/08/28/world/asia/north-korea-missile.html.

16   See Andrew S. Erickson and Justin D. Mikolay, 'Guam and American Security in the Pacific', in Carnes Lord and Andrew S. Erickson (eds), *Rebalancing US Forces: Basing and Forward Presence in the Indo-Pacific* (Annapolis, MD: Naval Institute

Press, 2014), pp. 14–35.

17 See 'Marine Corps Asia Pacific Realignment: DOD Should Resolve Capability Deficiencies and Infrastructure Risks and Revise Cost Estimates', US Government Accountability Office, 5 April 2017, https://www.gao.gov/products/gao-17-415.

18 See, for example, Carnes Lord and Andrew S. Erickson, 'Bases for America's Indo-Pacific Rebalance', *Diplomat*, 2 May 2014 and Carnes Lord and Andrew S. Erickson, 'Bases for America's Indo-Pacific Rebalance (Part 2)', *Diplomat*, 6 May 2014, http://thediplomat.com/2014/05/bases-for-americas-asia-pacific-rebalance/; and https://thediplomat.com/2014/05/bases-for-americas-asia-pacific-rebalance-part-2/.

19 See Joseph Trevithick, 'The Air Force Abruptly Ends Its Continuous Bomber Presence on Guam After 16 Years', *Drive*, 17 April 2020, https://www.thedrive.com/the-war-zone/33057/the-continuous-strategic-bomber-presence-mission-to-guam-has-abruptly-ended-after-16-years.

20 See, for example, John Grady, 'Entire Navy Tomahawk Missile Arsenal Will Upgrade to Block V', *USNI News*, 22 January 2020, https://news.usni.org/2020/01/22/entire-navy-tomahawk-missile-arsenal-will-upgrade-to-block-v; David Lague, 'Special Report: US Rearms to Nullify China's Missile Supremacy', Reuters, 6 May 2020, https://www.reuters.com/article/us-usa-china-missiles-specialreport-us/special-report-u-s-rearms-to-nullify-chinas-missile-supremacy-idUSKBN22I1EQ; and Kris Osborne, 'Why China and Russia Will Fear America's "New" Land-fired Tomahawk Missile', *National Interest*, 20 August 2019, https://nationalinterest.org/blog/buzz/why-china-and-russia-will-fear-americas-new-land-fired-tomahawk-missile-74871.

21 See Peter Ong, 'US Marines Experimenting with Tomahawk for Land-attack and Anti-ship Missions', *Naval News*, 17 June 2021, https://www.navalnews.com/naval-news/2021/06/u-s-marines-experimenting-with-tomahawk-for-land-attack-and-anti-ship-missions/.

22 See Bruce Klingner, Jung H. Pak and Sue Mi Terry, 'Trump Shakedowns Are Threatening Two Key US Alliances in Asia', Brookings Institution, 18 December 2019, https://www.brookings.edu/blog/order-from-chaos/2019/12/18/trump-shakedowns-are-threatening-two-key-u-s-alliances-in-asia/; and Gene Park and Mieczysław Boduszynski, 'Trump Has Damaged the US–Japan–South Korea Alliance – And China Loves It', *National Interest*, 20 July 2020, https://nationalinterest.org/blog/korea-watch/trump-has-damaged-us-japan-south-korea-alliance—and-china-loves-it-165164.

23 Some Chinese analysts have had this thought. See Sun Xiaokun, 'A Chinese Perspective on US Alliance Management', *Survival: Global Politics and Strategy*, vol. 61, no. 6, December 2019–January 2020, pp. 69–76.

24 Ian Easton, 'China's Evolving Reconnaissance-strike Capabilities: Implications for the US–Japan Alliance', Japan Institute for International Affairs, February 2014, pp. 17–20, http://www2.jiia.or.jp/pdf/fellow_report/140219_JIIA-Project2049_Ian_Easton_report.pdf.

25 See Emma Chanlett-Avery and Ian E.

Reinhart, 'The US Military Presence in Okinawa and the Futenma Base Controversy', Congressional Research Service, 20 January 2016, https://fas.org/sgp/crs/row/R42645.pdf.

26 Motoko Rich, 'US Helicopter Crashes on Okinawa, Adding to Safety Concerns', *New York Times*, 11 October 2017, https://www.nytimes.com/2017/10/11/world/asia/us-helicopter-crash-okinawa.html.

27 See Karl Gustafsson, Linus Hagström and Ulv Hanssen, 'Japan's Pacifism Is Dead', *Survival: Global Politics and Strategy*, vol. 60, no. 6, December 2018–January 2019, pp. 137–58.

28 See H.D.P. Envall, 'What Kind of Japan? Tokyo's Strategic Options in a Contested Asia', *Survival: Global Politics and Strategy*, vol. 61, no. 4, August–September 2019, pp. 117–30.

29 Motoko Rich, 'Shinzo Abe Announces Plan to Refine Japan's Pacifist Constitution', *New York Times*, 3 May 2017, https://www.nytimes.com/2017/05/03/world/asia/japan-constitution-shinzo-abe-military.html.

30 See, for example, Motoko Rich, 'A Pacifist Japan Starts to Embrace the Military', *New York Times*, 29 August 2017, https://www.nytimes.com/2017/08/29/world/asia/korea-missile-japan-pacifism.html; and 'Japan Is Alarmed and Outraged by North Korea's Missile Test', *The Economist*, 31 August 2017, https://www.economist.com/asia/2017/08/31/japan-is-alarmed-and-outraged-by-north-koreas-missile-test.

31 See Steve F. Kime, 'Reduce US Forces in Korea?', *Proceedings*, vol. 143, no. 6, June 2017, https://www.usni.org/magazines/proceedings/2017/june/reduce-us-ground-forces-korea.

32 See David E. Sanger and Gardiner Harris, 'US Pressed to Pursue Deal to Freeze North Korea Missile Tests', *New York Times*, 21 June 2017, https://www.nytimes.com/2017/06/21/world/asia/north-korea-missle-tests.html.

33 David E. Sanger, Choe Sang-Hun and Motoko Rich, 'North Korea Rouses Neighbors to Reconsider Nuclear Weapons', *New York Times*, 28 October 2017, https://www.nytimes.com/2017/10/28/world/asia/north-korea-nuclear-weapons-japan-south-korea.html; and Jonathan Soble and Choe Sang-Hun, 'North Korea's Alarmed Neighbors Consider Deploying Deadlier Weapons', *New York Times*, 8 August 2017, https://www.nytimes.com/2017/08/08/world/asia/north-korea-japan-missile-south.html.

34 The seminal contrarian monograph is Kenneth Waltz, *The Spread of Nuclear Weapons: More May Be Better*, Adelphi 171 (London: International Institute for Strategic Studies, 1981).

35 See James Van de Welde, 'Go Ahead. Let Japan and South Korea Go Nuclear', *National Interest*, 1 October 2016, http://nationalinterest.org/feature/go-ahead-let-japan-south-korea-go-nuclear-17897.

36 See Johnson, 'China's "Guam Killers" Threaten US Anchor Base in the Pacific'.

37 See Thomas Callender, 'Completing the Pivot to Asia', *National Interest*, 7 July 2019, https://nationalinterest.org/feature/completing-pivot-asia-65526.

38 *Ibid.*

Chapter Five

1 See John R. Deni, *Rotational Deployments vs. Forward Stationing: How Can the Army Achieve Assurance and Deterrence Efficiently and Effectively?* (Carlisle, PA: US Army War College, Strategic Studies Institute, 2017).

2 US Department of Defense, *Strengthening US Global Defense Posture*, Report to Congress, September 2004, http://www.dmzhawaii.org/wp-content/uploads/2008/12/global_posture.pdf.

3 Deni, *Rotational Deployments vs. Forward Stationing: How Can the Army Achieve Assurance and Deterrence Efficiently and Effectively?*, pp. 6–8.

4 See Alexander R. Vershbow and Philip M. Breedlove, *Permanent Deterrence: Enhancements to the US Military Presence in North Central Europe*, Atlantic Council, Scowcroft Center for Strategy and Security, February 2019, https://atlanticcouncil.org/wp-content/uploads/2020/04/Permanent-Deterrence.pdf.

5 See Clint Reach et al., 'Competing with Russia Militarily: Implications of Conventional and Nuclear Conflicts', Perspectives, RAND Corporation, June 2021, https://www.rand.org/pubs/perspectives/PE330.html.

6 See, for example, Scott Boston et al., 'Assessing the Conventional Force Imbalance in Europe: Implications for Countering Russian Local Superiority', Research Report, RAND Corporation, 2018, https://www.rand.org/content/dam/rand/pubs/research_reports/RR2400/RR2402/RAND_RR2402.pdf; Kris Osborn, 'Russia vs. NATO: Who Would Win the Ultimate Showdown?', *National Interest*, 16 October 2019, https://nationalinterest.org/blog/buzz/russia-vs-nato-who-would-win-ultimate-showdown-88221; and David A. Shlapak and Michael Johnson, 'Reinforcing Deterrence on NATO's Eastern Flank: Wargaming the Defense of the Baltics', Research Report, RAND Corporation, 2016, https://www.rand.org/pubs/research_reports/RR1253.html. For a discerning assessment made since the Ukrainian–Russian war began, in light of Russia's military performance, see Robert Dalsjö, Michael Jonsson and Johan Norberg, 'A Brutal Examination: Russian Military Capability in Light of the Ukraine War', *Survival: Global Politics and Strategy*, vol. 64, no. 2, June–July 2022, pp. 7–30.

7 Shlapak and Johnson, 'Reinforcing Deterrence on NATO's Eastern Flank: Wargaming the Defense of the Baltics'.

8 See Douglas Barrie et al., 'Defending Europe: Scenario-based Capability Requirements for NATO's European Members', IISS Research Paper, 10 May 2019, https://www.iiss.org/blogs/research-paper/2019/05/defending-europe.

9 *Ibid.*

10 See Henry Boyd and Bastian Giegerich, 'US Military Presence in Europe: Posturing for Global Success, Risking Regional Ties', IISS *Military Balance* Blog, 13 August 2020, https://www.iiss.org/blogs/military-balance/2020/08/us-military-presence-in-europe. Some do not agree that a heavy permanent presence is necessary for deterrence.

See Melanie W. Sisson, 'It's Time to Rethink NATO's Deterrent Strategy', *War on the Rocks*, 6 December 2019, https://warontherocks.com/2019/12/want-to-deter-russia-think-mobility-not-presence/.

[11] See Bryan Frederick et al., *Understanding the Deterrent Impact of US Overseas Forces* (Santa Monica, CA: RAND Corporation, 2020), https://www.rand.org/content/dam/rand/pubs/research_reports/RR2500/RR2533/RAND_RR2533.pdf.

[12] Igor Delanoe, 'After the Crimean Crisis: Towards a Greater Russian Maritime Power in the Black Sea', *South East European and Black Sea Studies*, vol. 14, no. 3, September 2013, p. 371.

[13] Igor Delanoe, 'Crimea, a Strategic Bastion on Russia's Southern Flank', Russian International Affairs Council, 18 December 2014, https://russiancouncil.ru/en/blogs/igor_delanoe-en/1588/.

[14] See Dmitry Gorenburg, 'Is a New Russian Black Sea Fleet Coming? Or Is It Already Here?', *War on the Rocks*, 31 July 2018, https://warontherocks.com/2018/07/is-a-new-russian-black-sea-fleet-coming-or-is-it-here/.

[15] See George Visan and Octavian Manea, 'Crimea's Transformation into an Access-denial Base', Romania Energy Center, 14 July 2015, https://bsad.roec.biz/portfolio-item/crimeas-transformation-into-an-access-denial-base/.

[16] 'Russia to Deploy 10 Strategic Bombers to Crimea for Snap Drills', Sputnik News, 18 March 2015, https://www.spacedaily.com/reports/Russia_to_Deploy_10_Strategic_Bombers_to_Crimea_for_Snap_Drills_999.html.

[17] See 'Here's Where Russia Will Deploy Nuclear-capable Tu-22M3 Bombers in Crimea (IMINT)', *T-Intelligence*, 27 March 2019, https://t-intell.com/2019/03/27/heres-where-russia-will-deploy-nuclear-capable-tu-22m3-bombers-in-crimea-imint/.

[18] See Dave Johnson, 'Russia's Deceptive Nuclear Policy', *Survival: Global Politics and Strategy*, vol. 63, no. 3, June–July 2021, pp. 123–42. See also Adrian Croft, 'Insight: Russia's Nuclear Strategy Raises Concerns in NATO', Reuters, 5 February 2015, http://www.reuters.com/article/ukraine-crisis-russia-nuclear/insight-rpt-russias-nuclear-strategy-raises-concerns-in-nato-idUSL6N0VE2RV20150205.

[19] See Henry Foy, Max Seddon and Demetri Sevastopulo, 'West Takes Putin's Nuclear Weapons Threat Seriously', *Financial Times*, 27 February 2022, https://www.ft.com/content/e12976cf-59be-414e-b90f-56875df79753.

[20] See Stephan Frühling and Guillaume Lasconjarias, 'NATO, A2/AD and the Kaliningrad Challenge', *Survival: Global Politics and Strategy*, vol. 58, no. 2, April–May 2020, pp. 95–116.

[21] For the conclusions summarised in this paragraph, see Boston et al., 'Assessing the Conventional Force Imbalance in Europe: Implications for Countering Russian Local Superiority'.

[22] Robert Dalsjo, Michael Jonsson and Christofer Berglund, 'Don't Believe the Russian Hype', *Foreign Policy*, 7 March 2019, https://foreignpolicy.com/2019/03/07/dont-believe-the-russian-hype-a2-ad-missiles-sweden-kaliningrad-baltic-states-annexation-nato/; and Michael Kofman, 'It's Time to Talk About A2/AD: Rethinking the

Russian Military Challenge', *War on the Rocks*, 5 September 2019, https://warontherocks.com/2019/09/its-time-to-talk-about-a2-ad-rethinking-the-russian-military-challenge/.

23 See James Hackett, Nick Childs and Douglas Barrie, 'If New Looks Could Kill: Russia's Military Capability in 2022', IISS *Military Balance Blog*, 15 February 2022, https://www.iiss.org/blogs/military-balance/2022/02/if-new-looks-could-kill-russias-military-capability-in-2022. The authors recognise that Russia's modernisation efforts have been skewed away from ground forces in favour of strategic, aerospace and naval forces.

24 Boston et al., 'Assessing the Conventional Force Imbalance in Europe: Implications for Countering Russian Local Superiority'; and Barrie et al., 'Defending Europe: Scenario-based Capability Requirements for NATO's European Members'.

25 See 'Fact Sheet: Atlantic Resolve', US Army Europe Public Affairs Office, 1 September 2019, https://web.archive.org/web/20200604022036/https://www.eur.army.mil/Portals/19/documents/Fact Sheets/AtlanticResolveFactSheet190804.pdf?ver=2019-09-05-071340-827.

26 See John Vandiver, 'US Tanks and Troops Headed to Lithuania for Lengthy Deployment', *Stars and Stripes*, 25 September 2019, https://www.stripes.com/news/europe/us-tanks-and-troops-headed-to-lithuania-for-lengthy-deployment-1.600424.

27 Boston et al., 'Assessing the Conventional Force Imbalance in Europe: Implications for Countering Russian Local Superiority'.

28 See 'NATO Response Force (NRF) Fact Sheet', Allied Joint Force Command, Headquarters Brunssum, https://jfcbs.nato.int/page5725819/nato-response-force-nrf-fact-sheet.

29 See 'US Military Presence in Poland', Congressional Research Service, 4 August 2020, https://fas.org/sgp/crs/natsec/IF11280.pdf.

30 For an argument in favour of developing intermediate-range missiles, see Luke Griffith, 'Biden Should Continue Building Intermediate-range Missiles', *Defense News*, 23 December 2020, https://www.defensenews.com/opinion/commentary/2020/12/23/biden-should-continue-building-intermediate-range-missiles/. On other options, see Sydney J. Freedberg Jr, 'Target, Kaliningrad: Air Force Puts Putin on Notice', *Breaking Defense*, 17 September 2019, https://breakingdefense.com/2019/09/target-kaliningrad-eucom-puts-putin-on-notice/; and Jerry Hendrix, 'Filling the Seams in US Long-range Penetrating Strike', Center for a New American Security, 10 September 2018, https://www.cnas.org/publications/reports/filling-the-seams-in-u-s-long-range-penetrating-strike.

31 See Robert M. Klein et al., 'Baltics Left of Bang: The Role of NATO with Partners in Denial-based Deterrence', Strategic Forum No. 301, Institute for National Strategic Studies, National Defense University, November 2019, https://inss.ndu.edu/Portals/68/Documents/stratforum/SF-301.pdf.

Chapter Six

[1] See, for example, John Halpin et al., 'How Americans Envision a More Perfect Union: A Common Path Forward for the Country', Center for American Progress, May 2021, https://americanprogress.org/wp-content/uploads/2021/05/MorePerfectUnion2021-report1.pdf; and Matthew Petti, 'Poll: Voters Care More About Ending Endless Wars than Confronting Enemies', Responsible Statecraft, 3 June 2021, https://responsiblestatecraft.org/2021/06/03/poll-voters-care-more-about-ending-endless-wars-than-confronting-enemies/.

[2] Jina Kim and John K. Warden, 'Limiting North Korea's Coercive Nuclear Leverage', *Survival: Global Politics and Strategy*, vol. 62, no. 1, February–March 2020, pp. 31–8.

[3] Christopher W. Hughes, Alessio Patalano and Robert Ward, 'Japan's Grand Strategy: The Abe Era and Its Aftermath', *Survival: Global Politics and Strategy*, vol. 63, no. 1, February–March 2021, pp. 125–60.

[4] See Stephen F. Burgess, 'The Changing Balance of Power in the Indo-Pacific Region and Optimum US Defense Strategy and US Air Force Strategic Posture', US Air Force Institute for National Security Studies, INSS Research Paper, 2016, http://www.usafa.edu/app/uploads/Burgess-Changing-Balance-of-Power.pdf.

[5] Yash Rojas, 'Ellsworth Successfully Validates Base's Long-range Strike Capability', Pacific Air Forces, 21 May 2014, http://www.pacaf.af.mil/News/Article-Display/Article/591360/ellsworth-successfully-validates-bases-long-range-strike-capability/.

[6] Dean Wilkening, 'Hypersonic Weapons and Strategic Stability', *Survival: Global Politics and Strategy*, vol. 61, no. 5, October–November 2019, pp. 129–48.

[7] Lee Jeong-ho and Teddy Ng, 'New US Military Bases in Indo-Pacific "Likely to Be Temporary" for Troop Flexibility', *South China Morning Post*, 30 August 2019, https://www.scmp.com/news/china/diplomacy/article/3025125/new-us-military-bases-asia-pacific-likely-be-temporary-troop.

[8] See, for example, Tanner Greer, 'American Bases in Japan Are Sitting Ducks', *Foreign Policy*, 4 September 2019, https://foreignpolicy.com/2019/09/04/american-bases-in-japan-are-sitting-ducks/; and Brad Lendon, 'China Could Overwhelm US Military Forces in Hours, Australian Report Says', CNN, 29 August 2019, https://www.cnn.com/2019/08/20/asia/australia-china-us-military-report-intl-hnk/index.html.

[9] Stephan Frühling, 'Is ANZUS Really an Alliance? Aligning the US and Australia', *Survival: Global Politics and Strategy*, vol. 60, no. 5, October–November 2018, pp. 199–218.

[10] Shawn Snow, 'MEU-sized Rotation of US Marines Starting to Arrive in Australia for Largest Iteration Yet', *Marine Corps Times*, 18 April 2019, https://www.marinecorpstimes.com/news/your-marine-corps/2019/04/18/largest-rotation-of-marines-to-arrive-in-australia/; and Seth Robson, 'Rotational Force in Australia's Northern Territory Hits Target of 2,500 Marines', *Stars and Stripes*,

24 July 2019, https://www. stripes.com/migration/2019-07-24/ Rotational-force-in-Australia's-Northern-Territory-hits-target-of-2500-Marines-1520535.html.

11 F. Gregory Gause III, 'Should We Stay or Should We Go? The United States and the Middle East', *Survival: Global Politics and Strategy*, vol. 61, no. 5, October–November 2019, pp. 7–24; and Steven Simon and Jonathan Stevenson, 'Iran: The Case Against War', *New York Review of Books*, vol. 66, no. 13, 15 August 2019, pp. 24–6.

12 The US Defense Department's technical distinctions between 'rotational' and 'forward-stationed' forces, and between 'forward-stationed' and 'forward-deployed' ones, are important. Only those units permanently deployed overseas (usually with dependents) are 'forward-stationed'; everything else is rotational, regardless of whether that rotation sustains a permanent presence or not. Almost all assets and personnel deployed to CENTCOM are rotational, including all the forces deployed to Iraq and Afghanistan for the long campaigns there, as well as the combat assets deployed in the Gulf states and surrounding seas. See deputy secretary of defense Bob Work, 'A New Global Posture for a New Era', speech delivered at the Council on Foreign Relations, US Department of Defense, 30 September 2014, https://www.defense.gov/Newsroom/Speeches/Speech/Article/605614/a-new-global-posture-for-a-new-era/.

13 See Franklin Spinney, 'Syria in the Crosshairs', *Counterpunch*, 27 August 2013, https://www.counterpunch.org/2013/08/27/syria-in-the-crosshair/.

14 Stephen Wertheim, 'The Price of Primacy', *Foreign Affairs*, vol. 99, no. 2, March–April 2020, p. 26.

15 See Alex de Waal, 'Assassinating Terrorists Does Not Work', *Boston Review*, 24 November 2015, https://bostonreview.net/articles/assassinating-terrorists-does-not-work/.

16 'Balkan Rumblings', IISS *Strategic Comments*, vol. 23, no. 20, 20 June 2017.

17 See Eric Schmitt, 'US Troops Train in Eastern Europe to Echoes of the Cold War', *New York Times*, 6 August 2017, https://www.nytimes.com/2017/08/06/world/europe/russia-america-military-exercise-trump-putin.html.

18 'Former Head of NATO: The VJTF Is Not Enough as the Russians Need to Be Deterred by a Real Presence', Ministry of Defence, Republic of Poland, 26 February 2016, https://archiwum2019-en.mon.gov.pl/news/article/former-head-of-nato-the-vjtf-is-not-enough-as-the-russians-need-to-be-deterred-by-a-real-presence-02016-03-18/.

19 See, for example, Helene Cooper, 'Biden Freezes Trump's Withdrawal of 12,000 Troops from Germany', *New York Times*, 4 February 2021, https://www.nytimes.com/2021/02/04/us/politics/biden-germany-troops-trump.html; and Henry Farrell, 'Biden Is Freezing Trump's Withdrawal of Troops from Germany. There's a Long History Behind America's Military Bases Abroad', *Washington Post*, 9 February 2021, https://www.washingtonpost.com/politics/2021/02/09/biden-is-freezing-trumps-withdrawal-troops-germany-theres-long-history-behind-americas-military-bases-abroad/.

20 Eva Hagström Frisell and Krister

Pallin (eds), *Western Military Capability in Northern Europe 2020*, Swedish Defense Research Agency, February 2021, p. 64.

21 'Press Conference by NATO Secretary General Jens Stoltenberg Previewing the Extraordinary Summit of NATO Heads of State and Government', NATO, 23 March 2022, https://www.nato.int/cps/en/natohq/opinions_193610.htm.

22 See John Vandiver, 'US Has 100,000 Troops in Europe for First Time Since 2005', *Stars and Stripes*, 15 March 2022, https://www.stripes.com/theaters/europe/2022-03-15/us-forces-record-high-europe-war-ukraine-5350187.html.

23 See Robbie Gromer, 'It's Time to Sharpen NATO's "Spearhead" Force', *New Atlanticist*, Atlantic Council, 21 March 2016, http://www.atlanticcouncil.org/blogs/new-atlanticist/it-s-time-to-sharpen-nato-s-spearhead-force.

24 Statement of General Philip Breedlove, Commander, US Forces Europe, Senate Committee on Armed Services, 1 March 2016, p. 13, https://www.armed-services.senate.gov/imo/media/doc/Breedlove_03-01-16.pdf.

25 Frans Osinga, 'European Security and the Significance of the F-35', Joint Air Power Competence Centre, October 2016, https://www.japcc.org/articles/european-security-and-the-significance-of-the-f-35/ (reprinted from the Norwegian Air Force publication *Luftled*); see also Marc V. Schanz, 'All for One in NATO', *Air Force Magazine*, 28 September 2015, https://www.airforcemag.com/article/all-for-one-in-nato/.

26 The BCT, which has a personnel strength of between 4,000 and 4,500, is the US Army's basic deployable combined-arms unit. It is by design a stand-alone, self-sufficient and standardised tactical force. The BCT's constituents are subject to ongoing revision in light of prevailing trends. See Daniel Vazquez, 'Is the Infantry Brigade Combat Team Becoming Obsolete?', *War on the Rocks*, 17 April 2020, https://warontherocks.com/2020/04/is-the-infantry-brigade-combat-team-becoming-obsolete/.

27 This may not always be the case; Sven Biscop, 'Battalions to Brigades: The Future of European Defence', *Survival: Global Politics and Strategy*, vol. 62, no. 5, October–November 2020, pp. 105–18.

28 Christopher J. Fettweis, 'Restraining Rome: Lessons in Grand Strategy from Emperor Hadrian', *Survival: Global Politics and Strategy*, vol. 60, no. 4, August–September 2018, pp. 123–50.

29 *Ibid.*, p. 131.

30 *Ibid.*, p. 134.

31 The esteemed journalist and foreign-policy analyst Walter Lippmann enunciated the concept during the Second World War. See Walter Lippmann, *US Foreign Policy: Shield of the Republic* (Boston, MA: Little, Brown and Company, 1943).

32 Graham Allison, 'The New Spheres of Influence', *Foreign Affairs*, vol. 99, no. 2, March–April 2020, pp. 30–40; and Evan R. Sankey, 'Reconsidering Spheres of Influence', *Survival: Global Politics and Strategy*, vol. 62, no. 2, April–May 2020, pp. 37–47.

33 Thomas Wright, 'The Folly of Retrenchment', *Foreign Affairs*, vol. 99, no. 2, March–April 2020, pp. 10–18.

34 Mira Rapp-Hooper, 'Saving America's Alliances', *Foreign Affairs*, vol. 99, no. 2, March–April 2020, pp. 127–40; and

Wright, 'The Folly of Retrenchment', p. 13.

35 Jim Garamone, 'Biden Approves Global Posture Review Recommendations', US Department of Defense, 29 November 2021, https://www.defense.gov/News/News-Stories/Article/Article/2856053/biden-approves-global-posture-review-recommendations/.

36 See, for example, Becca Wasser, 'The Unmet Promise of the Global Posture Review', *War on the Rocks*, 30 December 2021, https://warontherocks.com/2021/12/the-unmet-promise-of-the-global-posture-review/; and Dov S. Zakheim, 'A Disappointing Global Posture Review from Defense', *Hill*, 3 December 2021, https://thehill.com/opinion/national-security/583947-a-disappointing-global-posture-review-from-defense.

37 Garamone, 'Biden Approves Global Posture Review Recommendations'.

38 Richard K. Betts, 'A Disciplined Defense: How to Regain Strategic Solvency', *Foreign Affairs*, vol. 86, no. 6, November–December 2007, pp. 67–80.

INDEX

Adelphi books are published six times a year by Routledge Journals, an imprint of Taylor & Francis, 4 Park Square, Milton Park, Abingdon, Oxfordshire OX14 4RN, UK.

A subscription to the institution print edition, ISSN 1944-5571, includes free access for any number of concurrent users across a local area network to the online edition, ISSN 1944-558X. Taylor & Francis has a flexible approach to subscriptions enabling us to match individual libraries' requirements. This journal is available via a traditional institutional subscription (either print with free online access, or online-only at a discount) or as part of our libraries, subject collections or archives. For more information on our sales packages please visit www.tandfonline.com/page/librarians.

2022 Annual *Adelphi* Subscription Rates			
Institution	£922	US$1,705	€1,364
Individual	£316	US$541	€433
Online only	£784	US$1,449	€1,159

Dollar rates apply to subscribers outside Europe. Euro rates apply to all subscribers in Europe except the UK and the Republic of Ireland where the pound sterling price applies. All subscriptions are payable in advance and all rates include postage. Journals are sent by air to the USA, Canada, Mexico, India, Japan and Australasia. Subscriptions are entered on an annual basis, i.e. January to December. Payment may be made by sterling cheque, dollar cheque, international money order, National Giro, or credit card (Amex, Visa, Mastercard).

For a complete and up-to-date guide to Taylor & Francis journals and books publishing programmes, and details of advertising in our journals, visit our website: **http://www.tandfonline.com.**

Ordering information:
USA/Canada: Taylor & Francis Inc., Journals Department, 530 Walnut Street, Suite 850, Philadelphia, PA 19106, USA. **UK/Europe/Rest of World:** Routledge Journals, T&F Customer Services, T&F Informa UK Ltd., Sheepen Place, Colchester, Essex, CO3 3LP, UK.

Advertising enquiries to:
USA/Canada: The Advertising Manager, Taylor & Francis Inc., 530 Walnut Street, Suite 850, Philadelphia, PA 19106, USA. Tel: +1 (800) 354 1420. Fax: +1 (215) 207 0050. **UK/Europe/Rest of World**: The Advertising Manager, Routledge Journals, Taylor & Francis, 4 Park Square, Milton Park, Abingdon, Oxfordshire OX14 4RN, UK. Tel: +44 (0) 20 7017 6000. Fax: +44 (0) 20 7017 6336.

THE ADELPHI SERIES

ADELPHI 475–476
French Arms Exports
The Business of Sovereignty
Lucie Béraud-Sudreau
ISBN: 978-0-367-51145-6

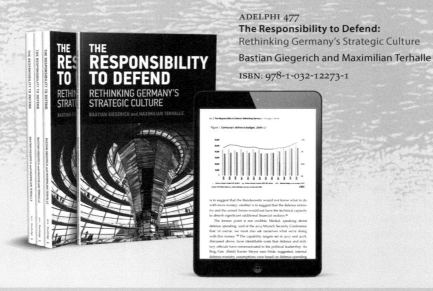

ADELPHI 477
The Responsibility to Defend:
Rethinking Germany's Strategic Culture
Bastian Giegerich and Maximilian Terhalle
ISBN: 978-1-032-12273-1

 THE INTERNATIONAL INSTITUTE FOR STRATEGIC STUDIES

www.iiss.org/publications/adelphi

ADELPHI 478–480
Asia's New Geopolitics
Military Power and Regional Order

Desmond Ball, Lucie Béraud-Sudreau,
Tim Huxley, C. Raja Mohan,
Brendan Taylor

ISBN: 978-1-032-18736-5

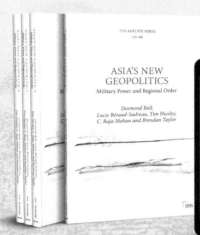

ADELPHI 481–483
**Japan's Effectiveness
as a Geo-Economic Actor**
Navigating Great-power Competition

Yuka Koshino and Robert Ward

ISBN: 978-1-032-32139-4

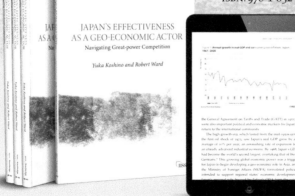

available at

OR